DEATH ON THE HILL

The Killing of Celine Cawley

Abigail Rieley was born in England but has lived most of her life in Ireland. A writer and journalist, she has covered some of the most high profile trials to pass through the Central Criminal Court in recent years for the national print and broadcast media. Her previous book, *The Devil in the Red Dress*, told the story of the Sharon Collins hitman for hire trial. She wrote about Eamonn Lillis's trial for both the *Sunday Independent* and *Hot Press*.

DEATH ON THE HILL

The Killing of Celine Cawley

364.1523

Abigail Rieley

THE O'BRIEN PRESS
DUBLIN

First published 2010 by The O'Brien Press Ltd,
12 Terenure Road East, Rathgar, Dublin 6, Ireland.
Tel: +353 1 4923333; Fax: +353 1 4922777
E-mail: books@obrien.ie
Website: www.obrien.ie

ISBN 978-1-84717-218-1

British Library Cataloguing-in-publication Data
A catalogue record for this title is available from the British Library

1 2 3 4 5 6 7 8 9 10
10 11 12 13 14 15

Printed in the UK by CPI Cox and Wyman.
The paper in this book is produced using pulp from managed forests.

Picture Credits:
Front cover image of Howth courtesy of Reflexstock.
Back cover image of Eamonn Lillis: *The Sunday Independent*.
Photographs of Celine Cawley, Celine Cawley and Jack Charlton, and
Celine Cawley and Juliette Hussey by kind permission of the Cawley
family. All other photographs as credited.

Dedication

To Michael, always.

Acknowledgements

Thanks go to my colleagues covering the Central Criminal Court. Without the cooperation and solidarity of the usual suspects covering the large details, it would be almost impossible to check the finer details. In this instance particular thanks are due to Aoife Finneran, Bronagh Murphy, Jenny Friel and Nicola Tallant. Thanks as well to Gerry Curran and Luke of the Courts Service Press Office for all their help during the trial.

I'd also like to say thank you to Neil Leslie of the *Sunday World* and Liam Collins and David Connachy of the *Sunday Independent* for all their time and help during the writing of this book. Thanks as well to Sarah Franklin whose advice was most welcome at a crucial stage.

To those who provided some welcome light relief and support: Al, Mercedes, Natascha, and the rest, as well as Mal, Charlie and Jude and Rosita.

I'd also like to especially thank my agent Ita O'Driscoll for her advice and support. Thank you to everyone at The O'Brien Press with a particular mention to my editor Mary Webb for her tireless attention to detail and my publisher Michael O'Brien.

Final thanks go as always to the husband, without whom I simply wouldn't get anything done!

CONTENTS

CHAPTER 1

An Ordinary Morning

Windgate Road snakes up the Hill of Howth, overlooking Dublin Bay. Addresses don't get much more exclusive. The houses that hide behind thick, high fences and electric gates are owned by people who are willing to pay a lot for a view and even more for privacy. Apart from occasional al fresco drinkers in the summer or teenage lovers looking for a quiet place to mate, nothing shattered the leafy peace – until two screams rang out one morning and a major crime shook the middle class complacency. The residents, who might not normally see each other from one end of the year to the other, would now have an excuse to stop and pass the time of day, to worry about the safety of their families and homes and the security of their comfortable lives.

15 December, 2008 started just like any other Monday

morning. Children were dropped to school, dogs were walked and the 'help' arrived to do the cleaning. In Rowan Hill, Eamonn Lillis had been up since before 7am. He had done his sit ups, as he did every morning, before heading downstairs to make tea and let the family's three dogs out to relieve themselves after a night indoors. As usual, he made three cups, one for himself, one for his sixteen-year-old daughter, and one for his wife, Celine.

Lillis was the only one in the family who slept upstairs. He had the master bedroom, with its sliding doors leading onto the balcony that gave the best view over the Bay. His daughter and Celine slept in downstairs bedrooms. It had been years since he and Celine had shared a bed with any regularity. Celine had a tendency to hog the bedclothes and the cold that she was currently nursing was making her snoring even worse than usual, but, in reality, the separate sleeping arrangements, developed in the earlier, happier years of marriage when work demanded early starts, had hardened into a cold, automatic habit of a relationship that was in decline.

On this Monday morning, however, there was no

outward hint of discord. Eamonn Lillis put a mug of steaming tea into the toy-strewn room his daughter no longer called a playroom, so she could watch some early morning television before school. He stuck his head into her bedroom to check that she was up and getting ready for school before continuing down the hall to Celine's room. There was no sense of urgency to the morning. Once his daughter had been dropped to school, the day was pretty much free apart from a meeting with their pension provider that afternoon. Since before Hallow-een, business had been slow at the film company he and Celine ran, so his main priority that morning was to pick up a set of Christmas tree lights. The old ones had blown, as tradition demanded, when they had been putting up the tree the night before. He paused for a while to watch television with Celine. She flicked impatiently between channels, he watched passively without comment. He would see his mistress while he was in town – something to look forward to.

After half an hour or so of watching the day-time televi-sion flick-pass, Lillis went back upstairs to shower and dress. He dressed casually, pulling on GAP jeans, a black polo shirt and a black v-neck jumper to keep out the chill of the morning. Before heading back downstairs he pulled on the pair of black Y3 runner boots from the wardrobe and grabbed one of his two Breitling watches from the bedside table.

Downstairs, Celine was putting together their daughter's packed lunch. He made himself breakfast, and when his daughter was ready, he dropped her the short distance to school. It was now around 8.20. At the school, he met an old college friend who worked there as vice principal. The Christmas lights were discussed and laughed about. The conversation was desultory, mainly about the festive preparations. By 8.30, he was on his way home. As usual, he stopped in the local newsagents to pick up *The Irish Times*. In every way it was a routine morning, but it wouldn't be for long.

Back home, the water pump was making a racket. Celine must have been in the shower. The dogs were milling around outside so he threw the paper down on the kitchen table and got their leads from the washroom.

The three family dogs were a boisterous lot who needed their exercise. Molly, the Newfoundland, was old and arthritic, but the younger two, Sam, the Rhodesian ridge-back, and Harry, the little cocker spaniel, had energy to spare. They were harmless, really, but passers-by were often startled by the frenzied barking behind the high wooden gate. There was a holly wood not far away and Lillis was hoping to find some sprays of berries to supplement the dusty garlands they'd taken out of the attic over the weekend. The wood was on the route he normally took with the dogs, up the hill towards Howth Head. Poor old Molly couldn't go much further. The years had got into her joints and if she was allowed to plod on for too long, the pain would hit that evening. He didn't get to the holly bushes in the end. It was only a short walk that day.

He got back to the house a little before 9.30am. Celine had dropped the bag of rubbish outside the back door for him to carry over to the bin area. She always did that. It was his job to put out the rubbish. He did a lot around the house. Celine was in the kitchen when he came inside after tending to the dogs. She was crossing backwards and forwards, emptying the ice trays and washing them.

The couple would have been married almost seventeen and a half years that Christmas but the cracks had started to show several years before. Friends and colleagues had noted the pair's contrasting personalities. Celine was never afraid to speak her mind, a larger than life figure in the lives of those who knew her. Certainly, she was a force to be reckoned with in the world of television adverts and had turned the company she had started, Toytown Films, into a leader in the industry. Her husband was known to be a dreamer, an artistic mind who was happy to take the back seat in the marriage and look after the home while his wife conquered the business world. Many commented that Celine obviously wore the trousers in the marriage – and, unable to hide her frustration, she had been known to speak to her husband so sharply in public that it raised eyebrows, but, on the whole, family and friends assumed it to be a happy marriage. The underlying truth was not so rosy, however. Certainly, the row that morning had all the bitterness and rage of two people who had once been very much in love but on whom life and living together had taken its toll.

The exact sequence of events isn't clear. It was an icy morning and the decking outside the kitchen was mossy. Celine followed him out of the house in her stockinged feet and they exchanged marital barbs. Years of resentment and petty irritations bubbled over and soon they were screaming at each other. One of them picked up a brick, a loose cobblelock stone left over from paving the patio. In one of the nearby houses, a neighbour, recovering from a late night with a family medical emergency, sleepily heard a high-pitched scream. The time was now just after 9.30am. A second scream followed in quick succession. In Rowan Hill, Celine Cawley was lying on the frosty decking, her blood pouring out onto the sodden wood from the blows that had split her scalp. The brick that had dealt the blows lay beside her as she struggled for breath in the cold morning air.

Her husband was nowhere to be seen. He had dropped the brick and hurried inside in a panicked cleanup that would end up putting him in the frame for murder. He was covered in blood after the argument had degenerated into hair pulling and face scratching. The blood was mostly Celine's, after he had hit her three times over the head with the brick in the heat of the struggle. It was everywhere. On his jeans and jumper and soaking through the winter layers onto his skin. At some point in the struggle, his expensive watch had gouged his wife, coming away with her skin and blood stuck in the metal links of the strap.

He ran upstairs and stripped off the bloody clothes and bustled around, ridding himself of his wife's life blood as she lay dying on the ground outside. He flung the clothes – the jeans and jumper and his boxer shorts and socks – into the new bin bag from the kitchen. Rubber gloves and tissues from his clean-up attempt outside went in the bin bag as well. It wasn't a particularly effective cover-up job. Panic muddled his thoughts, he couldn't think things through. In his frantic attempt to wash the last of her blood off himself, he left handprints on the sink of his en suite bathroom. Looking at his face in the mirror above the sink, he was a mess. A large lump was swelling over his right eye and three deep scratches ran across his cheek. It had been a horrific row. Celine was still downstairs, her blood spreading over the patio. As the blood flowed, her breathing slowed. Her heart, already under strain from the weight she had piled on in recent years, was struggling to cope with the lack of oxygen.

Upstairs, Lillis folded his black polo shirt and put it in with the clean clothes. He neatly placed his Y3 runners back with the other shoes. Logic wasn't working here; this was not the cover-up of a hardened criminal, but that of a frightened man. He took off the watch, realised it was covered in her blood, and hastily wiped the face clean. Still slightly damp from his frenzied scrubbing, he hurriedly changed into fresh clothes, unaware that he was leaving smears of his wife's blood on the inside of his sleeves as he dressed. He couldn't do anything about the scratches and bruises already vivid on his face, and Celine wouldn't look much better.

This was going to take some explaining. A robbery – that was the answer. It was the right time of year for opportunistic crooks to come in search of expensive Christmas presents. There had been a series of break-ins about eighteen months before. Rowan Hill had been one of those houses hit and they had lost some expensive photography equipment. A burglary scenario should silence even the most curious questions.

There was some camera equipment in a cupboard in the sitting room downstairs. That would do for starters. He grabbed a selection of lenses, a video camera, a film camera. There was a small suitcase sitting about upstairs that was just big enough to hold things until the coast was clear. The attic was still unlocked from taking down the Christmas decorations over the weekend. He tossed the black plastic bag containing the clothes and paper towels into the case, then dumped the camera equipment on top and zipped it up. He pushed it to the back of the attic space, covering it with his daughter's cast-off toys. The suitcase was hardly visible once he had pulled across her old dollhouse, a box of old books and some of her dolls.

He came back downstairs and only now went outside

to check on his wife. The scene there didn't help his sense of panic. Celine wasn't moving. He searched for a pulse on her wrist and her neck, as he'd seen on TV and in the movies, but couldn't feel anything. At 10.04, he finally rang the emergency services, his voice high and hysterical, gabbling as he described what had happened. This was the first time he had put the awful events into words, and it was a lie that came initially to mind, the instinct to divert the blame that was the strongest. His breath was coming out in ragged gasps, his voice tremulous, the accent rougher with the stress. And now, for the first time, he constructed the story he would cling to in the days and weeks that were to come.

Some guy had attacked his wife, he told the man at the other end of the phone. He himself had also been attacked. He had gone to get help but now he was back and she wasn't breathing, he couldn't find a pulse. The dogs were barking around him as he listened to the instructions being given. He was still panting to breathe. Celine had stopped breathing. Lillis took the directions for basic CPR, heard how to move his wife onto her back and tilt her neck to make sure that her airway was clear. As the calm operator talked him through what he must do, the emergency services were scrambled into action. Lillis attempted chest compressions and mouth to mouth, but it was too late for Celine. Even though gardaí arrived only minutes later, followed by the first ambulance, whose crew took over Lillis's amateur attempts at first aid, Celine could not be revived.

When the gardaí had climbed over the gate and hurried through the house to the patio out the back, they had found Lillis crouched over his unresponsive wife. He was almost hysterical at this stage. He was no longer making sense and looked as much a victim as his wife. As the house filled up with gardaí of various ranks, and not one but two ambulance crews, he added to his brief sketch of an attacker. He invented a masked man who had come with murderous intent, babbling the details as his cuts and bruises were tended to. No one questioned his version of what had happened.

Celine was bundled into an ambulance and rushed to Beaumont hospital, but it was to no avail. The strain on her heart had been too much after all the blood loss and she was pronounced dead shortly before 11am. Her husband was still being treated as a victim and the search was on for the masked man who had dared to bring violence to this exclusive neighbourhood. By evening, helicopters swept over the rolling landscape and a finger-tip search was being done at the end of the garden where Lillis's mythical thug had made his escape. Trapped into the constant repetition of his face-saving story, Lillis embroidered and embellished. As he answered the questions put to him by sympathetic gardaí, the story took shape. The phantom attacker began to take on the image of Stephen Larkin, the man he and Celine had suspected of robbing their house on that occasion eighteen months ago, although no such charges had been brought against Mr Larkin at the time or since.

Lillis constructed a story that painted himself in the best possible light. He told the police that he had come back from walking the dogs to see a man crouched over Celine on the patio, a brick raised in his hand. With no thought for his own safety, he had dropped everything and run outside to save his wife. But the attacker was too fast for him. He had come at Lillis with the brick and hit him in the face with it. That was where the scratches and bruises had come from.

It was easy to describe the fictional thug with such a clear picture of his former gardener in his head. Lillis told gardaí that the man was around the same height as himself; strong and wiry in build. He was a young man, he said, and even though he was wearing a balaclava, it had been possible to see, around the eyes and lips, that he was definitely a white man. He described his clothes in detail, with a cinematographer's eye. He was wearing jeans, a dark jacket and a balaclava – no, not a balaclava, more like a ski mask. On his back he had a rucksack with thick black straps, presumably all the better to carry off the loot with, and he had been wearing black gloves, so no fingerprints.

Gardaí began to be dubious. Balaclava-wearing robbers weren't particularly likely to be going about their business before lunch on the Hill of Howth. But they had no other explanation at the time and so a massive search got underway. The innocent Stephen Larkin found himself dragged from his bed and hauled in for questioning, while Lillis and his daughter were moved out of Rowan Hill so that gardaí could continue their forensic examination. 'Whatever it takes to get him,' Lillis told them.

By that evening, the media frenzy had begun in earnest as it became known that crime had entered the heart of Dublin's moneyed classes. The story immediately became front page news, and once Celine Cawley became linked to internationally iconic names like James Bond, Chanel and Vogue, it became clear that the interest was never going to go away. The first photographers arrived, and left with photographs of the sprawling four-bedroomed house.

Celine had been lying not far from the hot tub and its wooden cover was just visible from the vantage point across the garden from the lane that ran down by the side of the house. The rolling lawn of the garden led up to stables and a daisy-patterned, life-size ornamental cow statue grazed near the hedge. Within hours, rumours had started to circulate behind the scenes that the masked attacker was a little too Hollywood for reality, and eyes turned towards Eamonn Lillis, on the scent of yet another high profile wife killing.

For the moment, though, he was nothing more than a bereaved husband whose family and friends had gathered around him in shock and sympathy. Earlier, Lillis had rung the Toytown office to tell their staff his version of what had happened, taking the opportunity to further flesh out the character of the mysterious masked man. He said that he had heard Harry, the cocker spaniel, barking aggressively at someone; it must have been the attacker. By the time Lillis arrived at his brother-in-law Chris Cawley's house in Howth where the family had gathered, the news was already out that Celine was dead. The Cawley house became the hub of the family's grief and soon was busy with a constant stream of friends and well wishers.

When Lillis finally joined them after some hours spent being interviewed by the gardaí, he was accompanied by Celine's elderly father, James, a retired solicitor who had met him at the garda station. When Lillis's daughter heard him enter the house she came running downstairs from her cousin's room and into her father's arms. The outpouring of grief from father and child was witnessed by many, who politely stepped out of the way to allow this expression of loss more privacy.

The news reports on that night had all the details of the 'masked attacker', and Lillis rehearsed his story yet again to an audience hanging on his every word around the kitchen table. He even brought some humour to the otherwise macabre retelling of Celine's final moments when he described the pratfall of one of the emergency personnel who had come a cropper on the icy decking. That night, none of Celine's family questioned this account of the attack at Rowan Hill and saw Lillis as simply a grieving member of the family. They closed round him and his daughter to protect them from the media glare being directed their way, and prepared to stand by them whatever might come.

In a few short days their faith would be severely shaken as another, darker, scenario started to emerge and the finger of blame pointed squarely at Eamonn Lillis. But, on the night of 15 December 2008, few, if any, had the slightest idea that he was lying or that his marriage to Celine was not as happy as they presumed.

CHAPTER 2

An Unusual Match

Even from early childhood Celine Cawley was a whirl-wind of energy. She was the much loved third child of solicitor James Cawley and his wife Brenda. Born in June 1962, she enjoyed a seaside childhood with her two sisters, Susanna and Barbara, and brother, Chris, in the north Dublin suburb of Portmarnock. Her family was exceptionally well connected. Neighbours in those years included the broadcaster Eamonn Andrews, and her father was a good friend and business associate of media mogul Anthony O'Reilly, serving on the board of Independent Newspapers at one point. O'Reilly was also a partner in James Cawley's legal firm, Cawley Sheerin Wynne.

James Cawley was also one of the men involved in the setting up of the International Financial Services Centre

(IFSC) in Dublin. He was friendly with the Haughey family and was appointed by former taoiseach Charles Haughey to the Fianna Fáil fundraising committee. O'Reilly used to route his companies election time donations to the party through Mr Cawley, as a FF fundraiser.

Celine was a lively child and well liked. In an interview after her death, her friend and cousin, Juliette Hussey, described her as 'always up to devilment. It was always great when you heard Celine was coming over, you knew there was going to be fun.'

She went to school in Scoil Íosa in Malahide, then became a boarder in Claremont Convent Girls School in Rathnew, County Wicklow. Some of her happiest childhood summers were spent with her cousin in Hossegar in south-west France where Juliette's mother had a house. It was a happy childhood and a privileged one. At University College, Dublin she ran with the wealthy set, a tall, slim and strikingly beautiful teenager, with a natural confidence and poise. Those who knew her then described her as 'absolutely breathtaking'. An accomplished horse rider and yachtswoman, she was the kind of girl who turned heads and had no problem keeping their attention.

Towards the end of her schooling her life took a glamorous turn. Her discovery came while she was acting as receptionist in her father's firm during the summer holidays. A photographer, Tony Higgins, came to take some corporate shots and got chatting to her as he waited to do the job. Had she ever considered modelling? he asked her. She hadn't, she replied. He offered to shoot her portfolio and, in true fairytale style, the stage was set.

Somewhat to her doting father's consternation, she signed up with the Nan Morgan Agency in Dublin and was soon a hit. As always, she demanded that people took her as she was, even in that looks-obsessed world. Those who worked with her in those days remembered her forthright manner and relaxed attitude. Unlike other models of the time, who would turn up to shoots in full makeup and with carefully done hair, Celine was one of the first of a new breed who would arrive in jeans and a t-shirt and without a scrap of makeup on. She was never anything less than professional, though, the business sense that would serve her so well in later life was present even then. She was also exceptionally photogenic, as photos taken at the time show.

After three years, the Irish market began to seem rather small and she moved across to the bright lights of New York. When she first went over she stayed with John and Kay McEnroe, parents of the controversial tennis star who was at the height of his fame at that time. John McEnroe Snr and Celine's father had been business associates in the past and the family were happy to welcome the bubbly teenager into their home. She even dated their younger son, Mark, for a time in those early days.

Before long, Celine was discovered by Johnny Casanova of the world famous Elite Model Agency. That catapulted her into the big time. Contracts followed for *American Vogue* and *Elle* Magazine and she was soon hobnobbing with the glitterati of New York City. She became a feature of the diary pages back home, which eagerly followed her progress. With all the excitement of youth, she would reel off the stars she was rubbing shoulders with, dropping names like Bruce Springsteen,

Jacqueline Bisset, Ryan O'Neil and Bjorn Borg. But about those who she saw as more on her level she could be caustic. She once told the *Sunday Independent* in an interview that Brooke Shields, then the face of Calvin Klein jeans and three years her junior, was an 'airhead' and already getting heavy on the hips.

The work kept rolling in – big name brands like Chanel and Pierre Cardin – and she took to it with the same professional vigour that she had applied in Ireland, all the time updating the papers back home. On one shoot for Christian Dior in Paris, she had to pose with a bird of prey. She would tell the *Sunday Independent* excitedly:

'My heart did a somersault – it was an enormous falcon with beady eyes who was required to perch on my arm. He nipped my ear instantly, as if to prove he was as vicious as I thought he was.'

Celine was enjoying the jet-set lifestyle of the top model, but it wasn't long before the charms of New York started to pall. She transferred to the L'Agence modelling agency in Paris and continued her modelling in the sophisticated surroundings of the French capital.

But after a few years of the modelling life she was becoming tired of it. Her thoughts had turned to life beyond the fashion business and she was fascinated by the idea of acting. In 1985 she got the opportunity to experience the movie world for herself when a part came up in the James Bond film *A View to a Kill*. It was a small part; she is not named in the credits, merely described as one of 'The Girls'. Her task was to look alluring and make eyes at Bond, played by Roger Moore, as he passed her by at a party. After her death, grainy images of her looking doe-eyed at him circulated on the net. She was now sealed forever in the global consciousness as one of the elite group of Bond girls – but this was no speaking part and it was over in the blink of an eye. Even so, it was enough to give her a glimpse of what to do next with her life.

She took an extended break from modelling and went back to Dublin for a couple of months. It was then she met the international yachtsman Gordon Maguire. At the time he was running a surf shop in Howth and she wanted lessons. In an interview with the *Irish Mail* after her death he described her as a 'firecracker' who had more energy than anyone he had ever known. He fell for the bouncy free spirit with the exotic aura; the former Bond girl thing was already working for her. When she went back to London he visited her, but they both knew that it was just a passing fling.

She shared a flat with another model but was still bored with the life. She had decided that a more permanent move back home was in order if she was going to get out of the modelling business and into film. So she gave up everything – the jet-setting lifestyle, the celebrity parties, the exotic job locations, and even Gordon Maguire. They kept in touch for a while but eventually followed their own paths.

To pursue her dream, Celine would have to get back to square one. She had entered modelling from the reception desk, and in order to secure a start in the film world that she now craved, she was prepared to begin again at the bottom and crawl her way back up. She had done it once and she would do it as many times as was necessary. So she got a job on the reception desk of Windmill

Lane, the venue of Ireland's most iconic studios, where bands like Thin Lizzy, U2 and the Boomtown Rats had all recorded. By the time she joined, Windmill had widened its scope and was now host to a range of post production and commercial recording facilities, a far cry from its rather more humble rock 'n' roll roots.

Once again, it was while manning the reception desk that Celine caught the eye of a mentor, and one with a very interesting proposition. That mentor came in the shape of veteran producer and director Gerry Poulson whose company, GPA Films, was booked into Windmill Lane at the time. He liked the feisty twenty-something on the desk and took her under his wing. Soon she was his PA, and it wasn't long before she had proven her interest in the game sufficiently to get her first taste of television production.

So Celine embarked on a new career. Gerry Poulson had seen her potential and was committed to teaching her everything he knew. She quickly proved herself a tal-ented and resourceful producer in a highly competitive and male dominated world. Poulson was impressed by her ability to manage budgets, always a major concern in such a high pressure environment. She had an excellent head for business and usually managed to bring things in below budget. She drove a particularly hard bargain. Celine moved back to London and worked her way up through the ranks, cutting her teeth on shows that Poulson was involved in, such as the long-running television drama 'London's Burning' and the detective series 'Pulaski'.

But once again home was calling her, and a move back to Ireland was on the cards. She was still working as a producer for GPA films in 1990 when she went down to the yearly advertising festival, the Shark Awards. She was staying with Poulson and his wife in their house in Kinsale, where the festival was held, and it was he who introduced her to Eamonn Lillis one day in Acton's Hotel, the hub of goings-on at the festival.

Lillis was also a Dubliner. He had grown up on one of the pleasant, leafy squares of Terenure, on the southside of the city. Born in 1957, he was the middle child of retired army officer Seamus Lillis and his wife Mairéad, who was originally from Rossnowlagh in County Done-gal. Eamonn had two sisters, Elaine, the elder and Carmel, the younger. He had been a quiet, studious child, a dreamer who was a constant bafflement to his authoritarian father, Seamus, a former officer in the Irish Army transport division. Seamus Lillis was a meticulous man, the kind of person who did everything just so, who the neighbours could set their clocks by. After he left the army he put his skills to good use as transport manager at Beamish Crawford. He was second generation army, and, faced with a son who would rather stick his nose in a book, he was mystified.

Eamonn inherited an interest in historical wars from his father, but little else. His mural in the garage of the house in Wainsfort Park might have been of planes swooping over a vast landscape in his take on the Battle of Britain, but his school friends at Templeogue College, those that remembered him at all, recalled a quiet boy, slight and small, who would have his nose in one of Ian Fleming's James Bond novels rather than kicking a ball around with his classmates or the local kids.

Even back then he was always writing, but dreams of a career as a famous author never materialised. He had toyed with the idea of becoming a journalist, but any romantic notions of the daring hack were quashed in his first months at the course in the Rathmines College of Commerce, at the time the country's only college of journalism. Those that knew him then remembered a likeable teenager, sociable but with more than a streak of Walter Mitty in his makeup. James Bond had been superseded by Dirty Harry and Lillis hid his natural quietness behind a Clint Eastwood-esque façade. Once again, he was attracted to the image of the tough loner, the dangerous but romantic hero he would never be. However, journalism wasn't for him and Lillis left Rathmines without a qualification. By this time there had been a tragic upheaval at home, his mother Mairéad dying when he was eighteen, and over the next few years the family would drift apart. Both sisters found husbands in England and Lillis himself also moved away from Terenure.

After his shot at journalism hadn't worked out, he went back to college for a less limiting option. On the English

Literature course at UCD he found an outlet for his love of poetry and film. He made firm friends on that course. He was a good listener and a faithful friend who could be a rock in times of need. Some of the friends he made in those years stayed close for life, several even attended his trial and acted as character witnesses for his defence. It was with college friends that he entered into that other career which lends itself to the artistic but financially motivated – advertising.

Lillis put his love of words to work as a copywriter and enjoyed a certain degree of success with the advertising and marketing company DDFH&B, working his way up to the role of art director. But by the time he met Celine he was freelancing; once again his quietness and dreaminess had proved unsuited to the cut and thrust worlds he tried to fit into.

He had known Gerry Poulson for some time before he was introduced to Celine – the advertising world is a small one and in some senses an incestuous one. Poulson liked the now thirty-three-year old. He thought him charming and mild mannered and didn't hesitate to introduce him to his protégée. It was 1990, the year of Ireland's best World Cup campaign, and Celine had inveigled the Ireland manager, Jack Charlton, to coach a team made up of Irish advertising creatives. The idea was to match Ireland against the rest of the world from the assembled agencies, and Celine was in the thick of organising everything. Lillis fancied his shot at 'playing for Ireland' and so they met … and they got on very, very well. Arriving back at the Poulsons' house that night, Celine told her mentor breathlessly that she had just met the man she was going to marry.

Over the course of the festival weekend they bonded. Lillis had just got an Alsatian, and by some fortunate coincidence, Celine had just got an Alsatian/Rhodesian Ridgeback cross. The two of them happily talked dogs – it would not be the last time Lillis would charm a pretty woman with stories of his canine friend. They seemed an odd match. She was so vibrant, so bouncy and energetic, while in her shadow he might have seemed somewhat grey, insubstantial almost. He was drawn to the beautiful, confident creature before him and she was attracted to his quietness, the dreamy aesthete that was so in contrast with her businesslike pragmatism. He was someone who she could take under her wing and protect from the sharp edges of the world. As the festival came to an end, they decided to keep in touch back in Dublin.

Things moved quickly from there. The festival was in September, and by December they were engaged, with the wedding arranged for the following July. Celine was not accustomed to waiting for what she wanted and Lillis was old enough not to fear commitment. They married in the Church of the Assumption in Howth, then went back to Celine's parents' house for the reception. Her family liked Lillis tremendously and welcomed him into their hearts. And he happily fitted into the close, loving family niche they offered him.

He and Celine were an affectionate couple, although it was often she who took the driving seat in the relation-ship. She would pay at the end of a night out and was the one who arranged everything, as she had always done with her family. She organised for Lillis and her father to share their passion for military history on trips to the

Normandy battlefields or the walled town of Carcassonne. Lillis appeared to accept her tendency to take control. They seemed good for each other.

After they were married, the pair bought a small house in Sandymount and Celine was soon pregnant. But it wasn't long before there was a hiccup in their somewhat idyllic life. Celine lost her job when GPA closed down and was faced with an uncertain future as a freelance producer. Despite being pregnant, she approached matters with her customary decisiveness and, with the help of her father and brother, she set up the company that would make their fortunes, Toytown Films. She asked Lillis to go into business with her, but he preferred to continue his freelance career.

Working initially from home, Celine built the company up from nothing. Within a few short years she had made it the leading producer of television and film commercials. She based herself in Windmill Lane, where she had started, and surrounded herself with a small team made up of Emma O'Beirne and Andy Bradford. She called Emma and Andy 'the kids' and they, and everyone else in the industry, called her 'Mum'. She was a force of nature, a larger than life creature who swept all dissention before her and wasn't afraid to speak her mind. She rubbed some people up the wrong way, but if they needed to be dealt with she would just send in Andy Bradford to be the face of Toytown in her place.

Under Celine's guidance, Toytown won contracts with the biggest names in Irish advertising: Guinness, Carlsberg, Cadbury, Renault, Volvo, the list goes on. Toytown was behind the memorable ad that featured Irish soccer hero Roy Keane dressed up as a leprechaun to herald the entry of Walkers Crisps to the Irish market.

The skills she had learnt from Gerry Poulson came into their own as she negotiated the fiercely competitive and unionised business with ease. She had studied the business and expected the best of everyone she worked with, just as she expected it of herself. She was scrupulously fair but could be a hard taskmaster, although those who worked with her would say that this was simply to make people achieve their potential. When it was necessary to do a night-time shoot, Celine would appear at one o'clock in the morning to ensure that all the technical and transport crew would be paid before they went home. But those who were not doing their jobs need not expect to keep them, as she would not tolerate dead weight.

Over the years, she would periodically ask Lillis again to join her in the company, but for a long time he refused. It was only when his advertising work was drying up that he finally joined Celine. She welcomed him with her usual generosity, telling him that, with his love of films, he would make a fine director. His advertising contacts would be invaluable, she told him, and she could train him up as a producer, just as Gerry Poulson had once done with her.

Lillis joined the company, as a partner and shareholder, on paper at least, although the reality of his day-to-day involvement was somewhat different. He soon learnt that Celine expected the same high standards from him as she demanded of herself and everyone else. When he put his view forward in client meetings, she would think nothing of cutting across him and dismissing his suggestions abruptly if she did not agree with them. Many people who were sitting on the other side of the table in these meetings were surprised at the tone she took with her husband. Just as she had never dressed up to go to modelling appointments, so she expected those who came looking to work with Toytown to take her as they found her. This attitude extended to the way she addressed her husband. Her forceful personality threw his quietness into sharp relief, and Celine was not the one who came off well in the minds of some of those who witnessed their interaction.

In their private life, however, they still presented a very much united front, and life was good. After the birth of their daughter they had moved to Howth, and the success of the company enabled Celine to relive her happy childhood times in France with the purchase of a holiday home in Biarritz in the south-west of the country. Celine loved making their houses into homes and was a talented cook. Her parties, especially at Christmas, were legendary. As the company boomed, she showered her family with extravagant gifts. The parcels under the Christmas tree would include presents for each person from each of the Cawley-Lillis pets as well as from the couple and their daughter. Although she no longer went out as much as she would have in her younger, party-going days, she would still open the doors of their house for flamboyant parties.

In 1998, tragedy struck the Cawley family. Celine's oldest sister, Barbara, died from cancer. Celine had approached her sister's illness as she always did – by taking the reins. She went with her to every hospital appointment, and after Barbara had lost the battle, she turned her attention to those that were left behind. She swooped in to look after Barbara's husband, Rory Quigley, and the couple's children. No one in the family would ever forget how she picked up the pieces at such a terrible time.

It was in Celine's nature to look after people. She was a devoted and fiercely protective mother, determined to give her daughter a childhood as happy as her own had been. She encouraged her to get involved with Howth Yacht Club, where her brother Chris was very active, along with his children, and was always standing by with a sweater if the Dublin Bay wind got too cold. This lioness instinct to protect also extended to her husband. She would not hear a word said against him, and over the years, when he seemed to be taking a step back from Toytown, she would offer him other opportunities, trying to spark his interest. He might have felt the sharpness of her tongue on occasions over the years, but others saw her as his strongest protector.

If Celine had any idea in the last weeks of her life that her marriage was not in the peak of health, she hid it from those closest to her. She was her normal, bubbly self in those last weeks, ringing around the family, discreetly trying to air her worries about Lillis's cholesterol levels or organising a trip for him, her father, brother and brothers-in-law to go to see a Davis Cup match in Madrid. If she had known that he was hiding anything when he went off on that trip she did not let on. She was busy getting ready for Christmas and had started to make enquiries among Dublin's equestrian community about a new pony for her beloved only daughter.

CHAPTER 3

Betrayal

Despite outward appearances, Eamonn Lillis was not a happily married man. Friends and neighbours told the media after the trial that his flirting was well known. When Celine introduced him to her attractive masseuse at the Howth Haven Salon after he had complained of backache, he set off down the path that would eventually lead him into the arms of another woman.

Jean Treacy was from Nenagh, County Tipperary and belonged to a well known local family. Her father, Brendan, had been a Revenue Collector in the town and was respected as a local historian, photographer and musician. He had produced five books on local history from his collection of old photographs. Mr Treacy and his wife, Bernadette, were well regarded in the Dromin area of the town, where they lived. He was a former chairman of the

Nenagh Brass Band and a noted saxophonist. He had worked for the local authority for over forty years and was also a Civil Defence instructor. Of his three children, Jean was the youngest. There was an older sister who lived with her husband and two children in County Kildare, and an older brother, a secondary school teacher in Belfast. Jean was the baby, and the pretty one. By the time she was doing her Leaving Cert, in St Joseph's College in Borrisoleigh, her dark hair and almond eyes were turning heads wherever she went.

When Jean Treacy hit the headlines during Lillis's trial, there were many former friends waiting in the wings to describe her as aloof and somewhat 'stand-offish'. After school she spent a couple of years working as a lifeguard at the public baths in Nenagh. She often wore a swimsuit rather than the more usual shorts and a t-shirt and was known for the care she took with her appearance. Eventually, she moved away from home, but, after a five-year stint at marketing, decided it did not suit her. She started studying at night at the Galligan School of Beauty on Grafton Street in Dublin, and in 2006 she became a qualified beautician. She got a job at the Howth Haven Beauty Clinic as a therapist. It was a part time position at first, but after a month she was made full time and soon became a popular therapist. Celine Cawley was a regular client, coming to her for weekly massage sessions to smooth away the stresses of her hectic schedule. When Lillis complained of a bad back, Celine set up the appointment, and he too was soon a regular client. He liked his massage harder than his wife did and the deep tissue treatments eventually helped ease his back pain.

In contrast to the 'stand-offish' description of her by some earlier friends, at work Jean came across as a bubbly, friendly person who was adept at putting her clients at ease. She was engaged to Keith Fahy, a merchandising manager eight years her senior, and would happily chatter away with her colleagues about her upcoming wedding. She had big plans for a full fairytale day, including a romantic ceremony in Tuscany. They had got engaged in 2006, but not until she had spent months looking for the perfect ring. She wanted everything just so, and the ring had to be a 2carat brilliant cut solitaire in a platinum Tiffany mount; she even considered getting a similar style commissioned when Tiffany's prices seemed too daunting. Eventually Keith was permitted to propose, which he did at the winter solstice at Newgrange. They were planning to send out the invites in January 2009 for a summer wedding.

But even her impending marriage didn't stop Jean noticing Eamonn Lillis when he came to her for his weekly visit every Friday. When he was due to come in she would joke to her colleagues about her 'hot' client and make suggestions about what she would like to do to him. The Howth Haven is an utterly respectable establishment, with its discreet grey front looking out over Howth Harbour. Inside it is all subdued lighting, relaxing music and perfumed incense, designed to create an image of professional luxury. It's the kind of place where voices are muted and the magazines in the waiting area are all of the high end glossy variety, where the treatments are carried out with hushed efficiency for its affluent clientele. It could not be further away from the seedy image of 'massage parlours' that offer their largely male customers 'happy endings'. By starting a relationship with one of her married clients, Jean Treacy would raise the spectre of smut and leave the salon in the glare of unwelcome publicity that threatened to tarnish its impeccable reputation.

For an affair that would end up splashed over the front pages of so many tabloids, it started innocuously enough. On one of Eamonn Lillis's regular visits, in early October 2008, the conversation moved around to dogs. Once again, canine companions proved to be an invaluable ice breaker. Just as he had first forged a connection with Celine over a love of German Shepherds, this relationship too moved into new territory after a decidedly furry opening gambit. As usual, they had chatted as she massaged him and he was talking about the family's three dogs, as he often did. She asked if he had any pictures and he, in a 21' century alternative to 'come up and see my etchings', asked her to come out to his car and look at the photos on his iPod. So, when she finished work, that's exactly what she did. He waited outside in his car until she came out, shortly after 6pm. She sat into the passenger seat beside him and he showed her the photos of Sam, the cocker spaniel. Looking at his hands as they held the iPod, she noticed how nice they were, neat, unusual for a man. That evening she didn't even close the door of the car as she looked at the pictures. They were in the salon's car park, not some secluded corner. Yet something changed between them. Despite Celine and despite Keith, a spark had gone between the two in the car and things were never going to be the same again.

The following week he came for his appointment. The session went along as usual but there was a subtle change, a touch of electricity in the air. He mentioned that he had some stiffness in his shoulders so she turned him over to work on his front. She expected him to close his eyes, but they remained open and fixed on her face. He was looking at her so intently that she asked what he was thinking, suddenly self conscious. 'Nothing,' he replied, but he kept staring up at her. She continued kneading the skin on his torso and he kept staring up at her intently. Again she asked him what was on his mind.

Again he replied 'nothing', tapping the ball gently back into her side of the court and heightening the vibrations that crackled through the tranquillity of the treatment room, with its candles and essential oils. They were silent for a few moments. Then he asked her what she was thinking. By now, the sexual tension was almost audible. She reached down and took his hand. She touched his fingers to the soft skin on the inside of her wrist, where her pulse could be felt racing. 'That's what I'm thinking,' she replied softly, before dropping his hand as if it burned her and rushing out of the room without looking at him again.

The following Friday they met again for his regular appointment, and by now things had gone beyond the point of no return. There was no denying their feelings for one another. The passion could no longer be contained. They kissed and the emotion took hold. After that, the affair grew quickly in intensity. They would meet whenever they could, usually in the car park outside the salon before Jean went into work. She had a regular day off on Monday so on that day they would try to spend more time together. They were both swept away in the intensity of the relationship and slipped easily into the suburban cloak and dagger of the extra-marital affair. Most of the time they could only manage to meet fleetingly, snatching a few brief moments of 'accidental' meetings in the parks and car parks of Dublin. The Mercedes ML that Lillis drove had the legroom and tinted windows that made their secret trysts far more comfortable, and there was less likelihood of being spotted by someone they knew when they stopped to indulge their passion in the car park of the Pavilions shopping centre in Swords. Sometimes they would manage to slip further away on the pretext of walking the dogs that had brought them together. There was a day spent wandering around the grounds of Newbridge House and Farm, in Donabate, County Dublin.

One Monday, Celine had brought their daughter on a trip to London. Lillis took the opportunity to welcome Jean into the house he shared with his wife and daughter and took her upstairs to the master bedroom, where they made love in the bed next to the French windows leading to the balcony. After that, they found two more occasions to meet at Rowan Hill, the sense of the forbidden adding extra spice to the sneaking around.

Lillis was a generous lover. He showered Jean with gifts. They started off small enough, little tokens of their feelings for each other, but got larger and more lavish as the affair careered on like a runaway train. By now the couple were getting more daring. On their Monday trysts they would venture into town together. They went to pubs and even met a friend of Jean's in the Cocoon Bar near Grafton Street in the city centre. Lillis was bringing Jean to buy a coat in Brown Thomas in his latest extravagant gesture. Both of them would later say that the intensity of the affair was intoxicating. She would describe the madness as 'infatuation', he as a 'mid-life crisis'.

By the end of November things were beginning to reach their peak. After their fling was almost discovered on Jean's inadvertently left mobile phone, Lillis bought her a new one. She had been planning to get a new phone anyway, but agreed to the present. Lillis also bought himself a phone, a Meteor that he kept away from

Celine. The subterfuge was coming naturally to him.

Friends of Celine would tell the press after her death that she had been happy in her marriage, blissfully unaware of the betrayal on her doorstep. She was still going to Jean Treacy for her massages. By now, Lillis and his lover were texting each other regularly, as well as making several voice calls. With the security of the dedicated phones they could be even more intimate with one another and the texts that passed between them got increasingly suggestive. Jean even sent several saucy picture messages to titillate her older lover. In December the texting reached new levels. In the last couple of weeks of Celine's life, the lovers sent at least two texts a day. Jean would spend her evenings with Keith, planning the June wedding and organising the wedding invitations, but she would still text her lover goodnight at the end of each day. She hid the numerous texts she received. In December alone Lillis sent her almost 150 texts, over double her communications with him.

Lillis might have been good at hiding his infidelity, but the matter was obviously weighing on his mind. Much would be made of a note found in his room after his wife's death. In it he appeared to giving himself a pep talk, telling himself that Jean would never be his in the true sense of the word and that he should make the most of what he had. He would later claim that the note was the basis for a short story, and maybe he did intend to fictionalise his predicament, as a way of introducing some much needed distance into the intoxicating situation he found himself in. Both he and Jean were taken aback by the depth of the feelings they had for each other, but since she was still planning to marry Keith the following summer, a future was not something that was on the cards.

She knew that he was not happy in his marriage and encouraged him to find a resolution. She had heard firsthand how Celine would sometimes talk to him with a thoughtless abruptness. One day, when they were meeting in the Mercedes jeep, Lillis's phone rang. It was plugged into the hands-free system in the car so she could hear both sides of the conversation. Celine wanted to bring their daughter to the stables and asked if Lillis had the Mercedes. He told her that he had. Bring it back, she instructed him, in a tone of voice that Jean found unusually sharp; her back was acting up and the ML was the only car that was comfortable to sit in. Lillis responded meekly, allowing the sharp words to wash over him and not showing any reaction in front of his mistress, but the incident still stuck in her mind.

Jean was sympathetic to his marriage difficulties and helped him to prepare a 'Resolution List' for discussion with Celine that catalogued all the things he was unhappy with. Although Lillis later claimed that the list was discussed 'over a bottle of wine' with Celine, in the third week of December the affair was still going strong. On the evening of Sunday, 14 December, Jean texted Lillis to set up their regular meeting the next day. She had just got back from seeing Transporter 3 at the cinema when she texted him at a few minutes to 11pm.

'Transporter 3 good. Love Jason Statham. You staying home tomorrow? K going into the office for part of the morning so can meet you somewhere. Miss you so much. x.'

A couple of minutes later she texted again, suddenly conscious that she might have seemed to be too pushy.

'No pressure though ok baby. x'

Another couple of minutes passed before she texted again, with the practicalities of sneaking around.

'Well as usual I'll have to play it by ear but will contact you as soon as possible in the morning. Night my love. I love you infinitely. Sleep well. x'

But it would be almost a month before they saw each other again. The following day, Celine Cawley lay dead, and Jean's world began to explode as her work, her fiancé and the press found out about the affair. In the days, weeks and months to come it would become one of the most infamous infidelities in recent years, and would be presented in the subsequent trial as a motive for murder. On the night of 14 December, however, the lovers went to sleep in pleasant anticipation of the meeting the following day.

CHAPTER 4

The Net Closes In

Lillis couldn't answer the phone the next morning when Jean Treacy sent the first exploratory text at 9.44. When she texted him a reminder to bring the Mercedes ML jeep at 9.53, he was still running, panicked, around the house, cleaning up after the fight with his wife, as she lay bleeding on the decking outside. At 10.26 she texted him again, 'Everything OK?' By this time Celine was being stretchered into an ambulance, with paramedics still unable to find a pulse, and her husband was leaving with gardaí to help them with their enquiries into an aggravated burglary. At 11.14 Ms Treacy's worried message arrived unnoticed.

'Getting a bit worried now Babe. x'

The Meteor phone that Lillis had used to text sweet nothings to his mistress was lying unobserved in the bedroom upstairs. Lillis was now with gardaí at Howth garda station. He had given them his work phone to examine, which had been left out on the kitchen table, not needing to be concealed from Celine's sight. He had already told the ambulance personnel who treated him for shock, and Inspector Angela Willis, who had arrived to take charge of the investigation, that he had been attacked, and the full sweep of a garda search was in action. The garda helicopter swooped over Howth Head, looking for a running man wearing a balaclava. Lillis was keen to appear helpful and gave the details of his morning again and again. He did not know, initially, that Celine would not survive the morning. He stuck rigidly to his story of a masked attacker. Once again, Lillis said that he had dropped his daughter to school and then taken the dogs for a walk. He had been gone about twenty minutes. He had walked towards the summit of Howth Head but not the whole way, because Molly, the New-foundland, wasn't up to the walk. He arrived back home at around 9 o'clock, he said, but he wasn't sure exactly what the time was, he hadn't been checking his watch.

Celine had left a bag of rubbish out for him to put out so he did that, then headed into the house. That was when he saw him. He had charged out and grabbed the attacker, but the guy had run away. He had chased after him, but was too slow. He had gone back to Celine and found she hadn't got a pulse. That was when he had dialled 999.

The gardaí brought him through his story piece by piece. They asked Lillis for a full description. Lillis replied that the man was 'about my height, 5'11". Not small but not very big.' He had been wearing gloves and jeans, but Lillis didn't know what kind of footwear he had on. The guy was 'young, strong and wiry'. He had a rucksack on his back; Lillis said he could see the black straps coming over his shoulders. The house alarm hadn't been on, he told them. He had no idea whether the attacker had been inside the house. At 11.24 gardaí told Lillis that he could go and get changed into some clean clothes. It was OK, Lillis had replied. He had already washed at home.

Lillis told the gardaí he would have gone after the attacker if it hadn't been for Celine.

'Did he have a weapon?' they wanted to know.

'He had a brick,' Lillis replied. It was still up at the house.

Was it one of the bricks from round the house?

'I think so, yeah,' he replied, adding helpfully, 'there was blood on it.'

They asked him when he had seen the man.

'When I came into the kitchen. I saw Celine on the ground. He was on her. I roared and he stood straight up.' Lillis was full of regret. He should have roared out sooner, he told gardaí. He should have gone straight outside. The man had hit him a couple of times, he said.

'I was trying to hold him back, then I slipped and he ran off.'

The gardaí led him gently through his family background, the fact that his parents were dead, his sisters lived in England.

Lillis handed over the combats, t-shirt and jumper he had been wearing, with assurances that these were the clothes in which he had grappled with the assailant. He didn't mention that he had changed out of his bloody clothes, most of which were now in the suitcase hidden under his daughter's old toys. He didn't mention that the Breitling watch that was still lying on the bedside table in his bedroom was the one that had the blood traces on it, not the one he now handed to gardaí to forensically examine for traces of the mysterious burglar. He told the doctor who examined him at the garda station that he had been hit with a brick in the face, but made no mention of the injury to the ring finger on his left hand. As he took a break in making his statement, Lillis was handed his phone to call work and tell them he wouldn't be in. He spoke to Emma O'Beirne, and told her that Celine had been assaulted at the house. He told her not to worry, someone had told him up at Rowan Hill that Celine would be OK and the gardaí were going to contact his daughter and tell her what had happened. He did not know that at that stage the emergency doctors in Beaumont hospital were about to pronounce his wife dead. Gardaí took the necessary swabs and photographs of Lillis's injuries that might hold vital forensic evidence that would trap Celine Cawley's attacker.

It was not until almost 3.15 that Lillis finally sat down to make a formal statement. By now he knew that his wife was dead, but the panic had not left him and he stuck rigidly to his story. As he continued to weave the complex net of lies, the attacker in its midst ceased to be a faceless monster and took on a far more familiar guise. He gave the gardaí a step by step account of his morning routine. How he had got up at around 6.30 and done his sit ups. How he had made tea for himself and Celine and let the dogs out to do their business. He described how Celine had flicked through the morning television and how he had dropped his daughter to school and chatted with her vice principal about the blowing of the Christmas lights the night before. He described his stop off at the Summit newsagents to buy the paper and how he had returned home five or ten minutes later. The dogs had run up to the car as he had pulled up so he decided to take them for a walk. He told them how he had returned home to the bag of rubbish and had put it with the bins before going inside. His description of the attacker hinted at an even more sinister motive than a simple robbery.

'That's when I seen him on top of Celine. I don't know what he was doing. He was at her top. I charged out the door. I was roaring. He rose to his feet. The brick was in his hand.'

Lillis said he had fended the man off by putting his hands inside the other's elbows.

'I was trying to restrain him.'

His attacker had hit him with the brick and he had fallen back. It hadn't been a heavy blow. The gardaí asked him if the masked man had said anything.

'He didn't say a word. He was just breathing. Then he legged it.'

Lillis said he had no idea how he had hurt his finger. It could have been on the brick. His account blended the truth with the lie almost seamlessly. The description of the assailant was, if anything, even more detailed than the minutiae of his morning.

'He had a balaclava on him, a ski mask, one of those things. It was definitely a white male.' The man had been wearing black nylon gloves and had been in his twenties or thirties. He was holding the brick in his right hand.

'I assumed he was right-handed. I'm right-handed as well.'

He had seen the man running away to his left and had presumed he had hopped over the fence into the neighbour's garden. They had put up the fence after 'the last burglary'.

'Celine was on the deck on her side. I put my hands on her neck, trying to get a pulse. I tried her wrist as well.'

Lillis said he had never attempted CPR before. He was going by what he had seen in the movies. He had phoned for help and had been talked through the process. Help had seemed to be a long time coming, he said. The gardaí brought him back to the attack itself. How had his wife been lying when he first saw her?

'She was on her side, facing out from the house. He seemed to be crouching over her. He had the brick in his hand.'

What about the dogs? he was asked. Wouldn't they have attacked an intruder? Lillis was definite in his response. They weren't guard dogs. Once again the conversation drifted away from the attack. Celine had been wearing a sweatshirt and knee length leggings. She must have changed out of her night clothes after having a shower. They weren't planning on going into work that morning, he told them. They would normally have gone in between 9.30 and 10, but work was quiet at the moment. They didn't have to be anywhere until their 2pm appointment with their pension guy. He told them about Celine's background and family, how she had set up the company and how he had joined her about two years later as a partner.

The attack had been a complete surprise, he told them. There had been no strange phone calls, but they had been robbed before. They had their suspicions then, he said, getting the frame good and ready.

'Celine got a text message from our old babysitter saying this man was around again.'

Before the end of the day, gardaí were round at the house where Stephen Larkin lived. Larkin had done some landscape gardening work for the Lillis-Cawleys a couple of years previously. He was questioned about his part in the attack on Celine. Despite his innocence, it would be a long time before he would be able to get rid of the stain on his character as the news of his arrest lingered in local minds like a bad smell. Back in Howth garda station, Lillis was musing on his wife's reaction to finding a burglar on the premises.

'Celine is a fighter, a tough nut. She would have confronted someone. She wasn't a wallflower.'

Lillis wanted to know when he could go back home but was told it would be a few days yet. Gardaí were now investigating a murder, not an aggravated burglary. Lillis said he understood. He just wanted to see the perpetrator caught. His father-in-law had arrived at the station and Lillis left with him to go to Chris Cawley's house, where his devastated daughter was waiting for him. His family and friends had gathered round, all converging on the house in an outpouring of grief and sympathy. Lillis told them all what had happened, keeping to his story of the attacker. He would later say in court that he felt trapped, backed into a corner in the face of their heartfelt sympathy. He did not tell them the truth. Later that night he texted Jean Treacy, finally replying to her increasingly worried texts. He described his day as 'a horrifying day, a day from hell'. At this point his lover believed that he and Celine had been attacked by a burglar. The next morning she texted him, saying, 'I want you to know I still feel the exact same about you OK. I'll keep those appointments in case you need them. I'll see you at the funeral.'

That same morning, Lillis rang Detective Sergeant Enda Mulryan, to whom he had spoken the previous day. He told him he had remembered some things he hadn't put in his statement. The sergeant went to Chris Cawley's house and took a second statement. Lillis had decided to add even more detail to his account, filling in any awkward gaps that were likely to be seized on. He explained that he had realised overnight that he had left out an important detail. He had blacked out for a short time after he had been hit and fell on the decking.

'I remember seeing him turn and I passed out. Next thing I knew I ran down to see where he had gone.'

He explained that he hadn't heard any sounds of someone running through the woods to the left of the ornamental cow that stood in the corner of the garden. He commented that the masked man couldn't have gone round near the house because the area near the stables was like a bog. After checking where his attacker had gone, he went straight back to Celine, he said.

'I was trying to get a pulse and I had her hand to my face.'

Had his wife been conscious? the garda asked him.

'I think she opened her eyes. I don't know.'

He described his attempts to find a pulse.

'I put both hands onto her neck and left them there for a while. I couldn't tell whether I was getting her pulse or mine.'

How long had he left his wife lying there? It hadn't been long, he insisted. He had only gone halfway down the garden. He also embellished the description of his mythical assailant. He had been wearing a bomber type jacket, and the strip around the balaclava was in a contrasting colour, white or cream. In the days that followed, he rang the gardaí repeatedly to ask when he could get back into his house. Each time, he was told it would take just a little longer.

That night, Jean Treacy texted him again. It would be the last text she would send him for some considerable time. By the end of the week the Howth Haven Salon would have found out about her affair and she would have left her job. Already she was feeling the pressure. Her text read:

'Best of luck with everything always. You need to concentrate on [your daughter] and what's happening to you. To do this I don't think we should have any contact until things have calmed down (for both our sakes). I know you'll understand. Everyone is looking for a story. This is not an easy decision for me to make. Will be thinking of you every step of the way. x'

The garda investigation continued but questions were arising every day that Lillis's statement, even with the added detail, wasn't able to answer. The forensic investigation was already in full swing. Gardaí searched every inch of Rowan Hill, and, the more their enquiries progressed, the more Lillis's story simply didn't add up. At first they were looking for traces of the burglar. They did a fingertip search of the garden and the decking area, checked every inch of wire fencing around the spot where he was supposed to have disappeared into the woods. There was nothing. Not one fibre or hair, nothing that suggested the presence of another man. There was also the basic fact that burglars didn't usually strike, masked, in the middle of the morning when there was a chance that the houses they were breaking into would still be occupied. None of the inhabitants of Windgate Road had seen anyone remotely dodgy-looking on that Monday morning. There were people who had seen Lillis drive past on his way to his daughter's school. There were others who had heard the dogs barking behind the gate as they passed Rowan Hill, but no one had seen a man, with or without a ski mask, running from the scene of the attack.

The garda investigation started to focus closer to home. The search inside the house had thrown up some things that did not fit with Lillis's story of an intruder. There was blood on the basin in the en suite bathroom of the upstairs bedroom. On the bedside table, gardaí found the Breitling watch that Lillis had discarded, still stained with his wife's blood and tissue despite his attempts to wipe it clean. In the wardrobe they found a black polo shirt, also stained with Celine Cawley's blood. A pair of runner boots, put neatly in place at the bottom of the wardrobe, had minute flecks of blood on the white rubber sides of the soles and more considerable staining on the sole itself. It was the kind of blood spatter that would have resulted if the boots had been near the source of the blood when it was struck with some force. Gardaí also found a second phone on the bedside table, the one with Jean Treacy's worried texts on it. In fact, the texts and calls in the log of this particular phone were exclusively from and to Ms Treacy. Gardaí were beginning to build a picture of a marriage that was much less happy than Lillis had so far led them to believe. One of the most baffling finds in the search of Lillis's bedroom was also one of the most incongruous. Discarded on the dressing table, beside the loose change emptied from nighttime pockets and other detritus of everyday life, were two small bits of paper, torn from a notebook. Printed carefully on them in clear black capitals was a wistful list:

She will get that wedding dress

She will marry Keith next June

She will send out the invites in January

You will never be with her properly.

The only way you can be with her is to live here.

Think of the positives in the relationship.

You will never take her to France.

She will never share your bed.

You are running out of time!!!

By now, the gardaí were definitely interested in widening their enquiry. And when they searched the attic they discovered the suitcase that Lillis had hidden under all the childhood ephemera. Unzipping the Rip Curl case, they found a motley collection of camera equipment stowed on top of a black bin liner. Inside the bin liner, abandoned with an empty jar of pasta sauce and a probiotic yoghurt drink container, were Lillis's jeans and jumper, his socks and boxer shorts, a dish cloth, kitchen roll and tissue paper. All were heavily bloodstained. The security video taken from the Summit newsagents shop showed that Lillis had been wearing the clothes found in the bin bag and the runner boots from the wardrobe when he went to buy the paper on the morning of his wife's death. Forensic examination of the clothes Lillis had handed over at the garda station revealed more traces of Celine's blood. But the evidence wasn't on the outside of the jumper and combats, as would have been expected if these really were the clothes he had worn on that fatal morning, as he had claimed. The sleeves of the jumper were stained on the *inside* with pale, diluted blood. As if Lillis had washed hurriedly and hadn't dried himself before putting on the jumper.

The examination of the patio area yielded even more interesting nuggets of information. The large pool of blood where Celine had lain dying was not the only place where blood had been spilt. Forensic officers found a separate area of blood spatter, small droplets of blood that are sent flying when a source of wet blood is hit. These tiny spatters of Celine's blood were found on the white pebbledash wall between the sliding double doors into the kitchen and the living room window. There was also a long smear of her blood that looked as if a large spherical object, like someone's head, had been dragged along the wall. On the sliding door was a smear of Lillis's blood and there were droplets of blood that couldn't be identified on the step leading into the kitchen. These could have come from the blood that dripped from Lillis's ring finger after his nail had been ripped off. None of Celine's hair was found on the rough surface of the wall, but a single strand of hair was found on the blood-soaked brick. Due to the material used in the construction of the dark grey, cobblelock brick, DNA couldn't be extracted from the hair but it added to the picture of a violent struggle and was part of the evidence they were beginning to gather together as they built a case, not around an anonymous attacker, but against the person all eyes turn to in these cases, the husband. Then someone at the Howth Haven Salon came forward and told them about Jean Treacy, who had up till now been keeping her relationship with Lillis very quiet. They contacted her and she told them everything. Suddenly Lillis was looking a lot more like a suspect.

Lillis was still in bed on 20 December when the police

knocked on the door of his brother-in-law's house. Chris's wife, Sorcha, answered the door to them shortly before 7 o' clock that morning. Gardaí went upstairs to where Lillis was sleeping, and at 6.55 they arrested him for the murder of his wife. Lillis demanded to know what basis they had for arresting him, but they simply waited for him to get dressed and brought him to Clontarf garda station where the questioning began in earnest. In the car on the way to the station they asked him the name of his solicitor, to get the call in as soon as possible. Lillis didn't know offhand. He had never needed a criminal solicitor, and since his father-in-law, brother-in-law and sister-in-law were all solicitors it wasn't something that really came up. Someone had warned him that he might need one, though, he told them, and had given him a name and number. One of the gardaí scrolled through his phone, reading out the names and numbers in the address book until Lillis heard the one that sounded right. He was duly called and was to meet them at Clontarf garda station.

But before the questioning could begin, Lillis would

once again have to provide samples for DNA testing. He was fingerprinted and photographed. Not this time as a witness, but as a murder suspect. Lillis knew by now that they had found the suitcase of bloody clothes, and yet when he finally sat down to be interviewed shortly before 11am, he was still clinging to the story of the intruder for all he was worth. He had spoken with his solicitor by this time and was determined to take his advice. When the two gardaí conducting the interview reminded him of his earlier statements and his cooperation up to this point, Lillis replied doggedly:

'My solicitor told me to say nothing so I am not going to answer any questions.'

The gardaí went straight to the first inconsistency. Was he aware there was video footage showing him buying the paper in the Summit newsagents?

'No comment.'

They had the video – it showed him wearing different clothes to the ones he had said he was wearing, they explained. Did he have anything to say to that?

Lillis replied quickly, breaking out of his no 'comment'

stance for long enough to add a detail to his story. He had got changed before he took the dogs for a walk, he said. It was muddy up the Head so he had changed into combats and walking boots. Where had he got changed? the gardaí asked. In his bedroom upstairs, he replied. Then he had brought his jeans and the jumper he'd been wearing downstairs. He had left the jeans in the wash-room and thrown the jumper over the back of a chair in the kitchen. The black and white runner boots he had been wearing he left either in the kitchen or on the stairs. He had also brought down his t-shirt and left it folded up on the stairs. He had got his walking boots from the washroom and had gone out to take the dogs for a walk. He was asked how long he had been gone. Twenty minutes, half an hour max, came the reply. Molly couldn't go right up to the top.

'Her shoulder's gone.'

Had he seen Celine while he was getting changed?

'No, the pump was going. It's a noisy old bugger.' He explained that the house was up so high that the water pressure was always a problem. If the pump was going

Celine would have been in the shower or flushing the loo. Why hadn't he mentioned this before?

'To be honest, I didn't remember it at the time. I remember it now.'

At 11.45 his solicitor rang and Lillis had a conversation with him. Then the interview resumed. No one had seen him going for a walk, they told him. Was that unusual? Lillis dismissed the suggestion. He had definitely gone for a walk. The gardaí kept pressing him. If he had changed his clothes the way he said, then the clothes he had been wearing definitely shouldn't have had blood on them, should they? Lillis didn't answer. What about the phone he had given them. Was it the only one he had? There were a couple of spares, he told them, for back up. They turned to his marriage. How had his relationship been with his wife?

'Our relationship on a professional and personal level was very, very close. We were very good friends. She was a tower of strength to me.'

Finally the gardaí laid their cards on the table. Detective Sergeant Gary Kelly set out the situation. They knew it had all been a tragic accident.

'There's no point in beating about the bush here. It's quite obvious you just lost your head and flipped that morning. Everyone we've spoken to says you were a nice, gentle, caring soul.'

'There's something I want to say. I want to talk to my solicitor first.'

'Tell the truth.'

'I didn't kill her, I swear before God. I couldn't do it to Celine.'

'Did you love Celine?'

'God, yes.'

'Did you have an affair?'

'I never had an affair.'

They told him they knew he had regular appointments at the Howth Haven Salon. He usually had a back massage.

'Mostly it's a girl called Jean does it,' he offered. 'Celine goes down there as well.'

He would not admit to an affair.

'I don't see the relevance to this.'

'Was Jean ever in your house?'

'No.'

'Was she ever in your car?'

'Once, a month ago. I showed her a photo of my dog Sam. It was on my iPod.'

'Did you go anywhere with her?'

'No.'

'Have you had sex with her?'

'God, No!'

The gardaí kept trying to break his resolve but he kept denying the affair. Had he ever met Jean Treacy with a friend in a coffee shop in town?

'We did meet by accident, but we never had sex.'

Didn't they meet more often than that, the guards suggested. They had gone to Newbridge House, to the Pavilions in Swords...

'I may have seen her once there.'

What about the phone messages? There had been some, he agreed reluctantly, just to confirm appointments. Then they told him they had spoken to Jean Treacy.

'What did she say?'

'She said she's been having an affair with you for the past ten weeks and that she's been in your house three times,' came the reply.

She had also described that moment in the salon when she had put her hand on his wrist, and that the next time they had met they had kissed in one of the treatment rooms.

'No comment,' was all Lillis would say.

'The first time you had sex was in your house on a Monday, her day off. She thinks Celine and your daughter were in London,' they said. 'You bought her a phone and texted every day. We have the phone.'

'No comment,' was the only reply.

'Were you not happy in your marriage?'

'No comment.' Then he broke. 'I did have an affair, but it has absolutely nothing to do with this.'

He and Celine had some problems, but they had got through them.

'I had a resolution list and we worked it out.'

The list had been about what he felt was wrong with

his life, he explained, how he saw himself and where he would like to be.

'We sat down one night with a bottle of wine. By the end of it, it was very therapeutic.'

'Were you infatuated with Jean?' they asked.

'I suppose it was some kind of mid-life crisis.'

He denied ever wanting to leave his wife over Ms Treacy. He wouldn't break up the family. They told him they had found the notes on the dressing table in his bedroom. Were they about his relationship with Jean Treacy?

'That would be a reasonable assumption.'

The gardaí's frustration at his continuing lack of comment was beginning to show. They started goading him. He and Celine had a sexless marriage, they suggested. It was an arrangement that suited both of them. The details in the notes were about him. He was insanely jealous of his young lover.

'I don't do jealous,' replied Lillis stubbornly.

They knew he was going to meet her that morning, they told him. Had Celine found out about the affair?

'No.'

'Did you have sex in your bedroom with Jean?'

'I don't want to talk about this,' Lillis replied. 'I want to see my solicitor.'

Later that afternoon he had further interviews. This time the guards showed him the video from the Summit newsagents. Did he want to make a comment?

'I saw myself go into the shop and buy a paper. At least, it looked like me.'

They showed him the footage from a different angle. Was that him as well?

'I couldn't say for sure that person was me. I couldn't recognise myself,' Lillis replied after watching the grainy images.

The person in the pictures was wearing jeans and a dark top. He had on black trainers with white trim.

'That could or could not be me. I couldn't really say.'

They pressed him further, but Lillis was firm.

'My solicitor told me to say nothing.'

But the video showed him wearing different clothes to the ones he had said he was wearing, the guards pointed out.

'I'm not denying I bought a paper that morning.'

He had obviously been wearing other clothes, they insisted. He had changed into the ones he had given gardaí. Lillis told them had no comment to make on that subject. His solicitor had told him not to say anything. Eventually he told them that he had changed but that he had left his clothes downstairs. They asked him what kind of jeans he usually wore. Lillis listed off the brands: Timberland, Gap, Armani or Hugo Boss. The jeans in the black bin liner he had stowed in the attic were Gap. What about the t-shirt, they asked him. That would have been Gap. It had been. The black and white runner boots he finally conceded were made by Y3. He had got changed and thrown his jumper over the back of the chair in the living room. He had changed quietly, he told them, 'because if the dogs hear you changing shoes there's a general sense of hysteria.' The guards asked him again when he had gone on his walk. It had been sometime around 9 am, he told them. And when had he come back? He replied that that would have been around 9.30. They asked him about his watch. The watch he had given them was a Breitling watch. Had he any other watches? He had another Breitling, he told them. They asked him if the masked man had left while he had lost consciousness. Yes, he agreed. He had heard Harry, the cocker spaniel, barking inside the house, an 'aggressive nasty barking'.

'I paid no heed to it.'

On the map they gave him he showed them where Celine had been lying, then indicated his route up and down the garden in pursuit of the fictional attacker. It was now almost 5 o'clock. Lillis had been in custody for around ten hours. He complained that he was getting a headache and a doctor was sent for, to prescribe painkillers. As they waited for the doctor to arrive, the questioning continued. What had he done when he got home from the walk? He explained that he had let the two younger dogs off their leashes. Molly had plodded on behind. The gate was on a sensor so it opened automatically when she finally made her way to the house a few moments later. He put Xs on the map where Molly had lain down in her usual place and where he had been standing when he had seen the attacker looming over Celine. He marked where he stood when the attacker came for him with the brick. There was one issue they kept coming back to; the one major gap in his story. If he had come back from his walk at 9.30 and had seen his wife's attacker, why had he only called the emergency services at 10.02? What had happened during that missing half hour? He had passed out, he repeated. He didn't know how long for. Then he had gone back to her and held her hand up to his face.

'I was kissing her hand. I held her hand up to my face. I saw her hands open. I felt her hand clench.'

Only then did he call 999. The gardaí told him they had a witness statement from a neighbour who had heard two screams at around 9.30, the time he said he came back from his walk. Was he absolutely sure about the clothes he had been wearing? Lillis clung to his story. The guards were getting frustrated. They had his watch and his clothes – stained with his wife's blood. Lillis wouldn't budge. They closed in on the other big inconsistency. If the attacker had been wearing gloves, how had he managed to scratch Lillis on the face? Lillis changed his story yet again, he was obviously thinking furiously.

'That was Celine. I held her hand up to my face. I was kissing her hand. I pulled her hand down. I didn't even know there were marks there.'

He was granted a brief rest from the relentless questioning as the doctor arrived with the paracetemol. The interview continued after a break of about half an hour. The guards jumped straight in with questions about why the dogs had failed to attack the intruder. Lillis came back immediately with an answer.

'Molly's very laid back. Sam, the Rhodesian ridgeback, is very cowardly.'

He added that Harry, the cocker spaniel, had clearly come into the house at some point and had been barking nastily but he couldn't explain why he hadn't run through the open door. The guards returned to the subject of the note they found in his bedroom. They read out a few lines:

'You will never take her to France

She will never share your bed.

You are running out of time.'

'It's the basis of a short story I was writing,' explained Lillis. 'I do writing. I used to be a copywriter. You may have noticed a chapter I'm writing about a dog.'

The story, he said, was notes on a doomed love affair.

'Based on your love affair?'

'Well yes, on experience,' he admitted. He had started to write it four or five weeks ago.

The guards didn't accept his explanation. They knew he and Celine slept in different rooms, they told him. It had started when their daughter was a baby, he responded, 'rather than having the two of us fucked'. After a while it had become a habit.

'Celine always grabbed the duvet,' he said. They were both difficult to sleep with.

'If the marriage was so good, why did you have an affair?' the detectives asked him.

'Call it a mid-life attraction.'

Once again they wanted to know about the scratch marks to his neck. It had been Celine, he insisted.

'I thought she was still alive.'

She hadn't scraped him, he said, he had been holding her hand to his face. She had very sharp nails. The guards pointed out that her nails had been short. They were very strong though, he replied. He had often remarked about it to her. But on the day itself he had told them that the scratches came from the attacker, they queried. It was strange that there was not one drop of blood along the route he had said the attacker had taken. According to his account, he had fought with Lillis and had been standing over Celine when he hit her. Had the intruder gone back inside the house? In the face of another glaring gap, Lillis once again changed his story.

'I have a suspicion there wasn't one person in the house, but two. There could have been two people. It would explain why Harry was barking.'

They wanted to know why he had so little blood on him. He had been close enough to the attacker to grab at him and the attacker had been swinging a brick. Lillis replied that he hadn't been near his wife's head and he had washed his hands before he called 999.

'You are telling me your wife was lying dying and you

took time to wash you hands?' the questioning garda asked him incredulously.

'It was instinctive.'

He went on that whoever had been in the house, whoever Harry was barking at, had probably taken the jeans from the chair in the kitchen.

'You told us the jeans were in the washroom.'

'They were definitely on the chair.'

The suggestion was that his abandoned jeans had been used by the phantom assailant to wipe up his wife's blood.

The guards' frustrations were clearly showing.

'Was it more important to have clean hands than your wife's health or life?' they asked sharply.

'I think that's an unfair observation.'

Once again both sides took a break from the intense questioning. It was approaching 8 o'clock before Lillis found himself back in the interview room. The gardaí showed him the physical evidence they had found at Rowan Hill. Lillis looked at the items as they were put in front of him. Even when faced with his clothes that were soaked with his wife's blood, he clung desperately to his story of a masked attacker. They showed him the runner boots with the flecks of blood on the sides. They had been found in the bedroom, they told him.

'That's impossible. They were in the kitchen ... I was wearing them that morning before I went for a walk. There's no way they could be in the bedroom.'

They showed him the Breitling watch from his bedside table. When had he last worn it? On Saturday, came the adamant reply, definitely Saturday. He had left it on the kitchen windowsill beside his wallet. Next they produced a red brick, wrapped in a blue and white tea towel. It had been one of the more baffling finds from the house. Did he recognise it? He had been using it to prop up a ceramic cow while he fixed its broken horn. There had been a few bricks lying around outside the kitchen door so he had brought it inside. Had he wrapped it in a tea cloth? No, he replied. They showed him the blood-covered brick they had found next to Celine. Did he recognise that? It looked like the same brick used in the attack, he said. Had he handled it? He had picked it up at one stage when he was beside Celine, he replied. After he had come to. Next they produced the suitcase. Yes he recognised that, he said, it was one of their Rip Curl bags. They opened it. Did he recognise the camera equipment? Yes, it all belonged to either himself or Celine. It was kept in the cupboard in the living room. They showed him the black bin bag. That was the one he had left on the kitchen table, he offered. He had been tidying up the kitchen. The jeans looked like his, they were Gap. The pair of Abercrombie & Fitch underpants might be his as well. They were all either in the kitchen or downstairs in the washroom. They showed him the pair of blue rubber gloves, still wet with water and Celine's blood. Did he recognise those? Absolutely not, he replied quickly. They showed him a pair of black Thinsulate men's gloves. Did they look familiar? He had left those on the kitchen table, he said, he was going to de-poo the garden after the dogs. He had an answer for everything they showed him, or an outright denial. Even when shown the bloody jeans, he clung to the story that they had been used by some balaclava-wearing thug to mop up the blood left by their crime. The guards were incredulous.

'Do you still say an intruder killed Celine?'

'I have no comment.'

His DNA had been found on the clothes that were covered in Celine's blood. His blood had been found staining the neck of the polo shirt. The jumper also had his DNA and hers, and nothing belonging to any third party. They told him they had found his wife's diluted blood on the top he had handed into gardaí on 15 December. His shoes were splashed with his wife's blood.

'I was out at the time and I wasn't even wearing them.'

He wouldn't be shaken. The gardaí kept showing him the bloody evidence and pointing out the impossibility of the story he was telling them. But Lillis didn't deviate from his story.

'I have some definite ideas but my solicitor has warned me not to discuss them with the guards.'

Detective Pat Flood, who was the garda currently interviewing him, said to Lillis:

'This is the moment that you could turn it around. I'm appealing to you as a father, as a man, as a human being.

Nobody has said you were a nasty bloke. Everybody has said you are a decent, soft bloke. There has to be an explanation.' He continued, 'Shit happens, people fuck up. We just want to hear the truth. People are in pain. Stop it.'

Lillis stuck to his story. 'I am telling the truth.'

The interview paused a short time later, but only for a brief break. Lillis opted to continue the questioning through the night rather than going to rest in his cell. Detective Garda Paul Donoghue took over the questioning. He went straight to the point.

'Did you murder your wife, Celine?'

'On the advice of my solicitor, no comment.'

The garda didn't let up.

'It's my belief you murdered you wife last Monday by battering her head in with a concrete brick.'

Lillis still refused to comment. The garda changed tack.

'Was your wife a dominant person, slightly on the bullying side?'

'No.'

'Was you wife paid more than you in the business?'

'No comment.'

They wanted to know why he hadn't mentioned blacking out when he was examined by a doctor in Howth garda station on 15 December

'He wasn't very helpful, I must say.' Lillis replied. 'I'm sure I told him. That day was very confusing.'

Detective Donoghue circled back to Celine. She had been described as a strong, dominant, opinionated person, he told Lillis. People had said that it was a sexless marriage. He was her lapdog; she would regularly shout at him to come here, do that. He only earned €100,000 compared to her €500,000.

'You met a 31-year-old girl who wanted to have sex with you in exciting places, in the car in the Pavilions in Swords, in the same house you shared with your wife while she was away.'

'No comment,' came the response.

'You have shown very little emotion,' the garda said to him, adding that his story of a burglar was simply a 'cock and bull story'.

'Burglars run when they are disturbed. We deal with

them all the time.'

Had he had a row with his wife? the garda asked, and picked up the brick and hit her over the head with it until she died in front of him?

'No comment.'

Was he suggesting that his clothes had walked themselves up to the attic or that someone had brought them up there?

'My solicitor told me not to discuss this.'

Had his wife scratched him deliberately, the detective asked, when they fought?

'She had very sharp nails. Her nails probably cut me on the forehead. There used to be a gesture we had where we would touch each other on the face.'

'What would that gesture mean?'

'Love.'

But they didn't believe him. He was running out of excuses, they said. Why would burglars have stashed stuff in the attic?

'They wouldn't be caught going down the road with it,' Lillis suggested.

'He stashed it in the attack and said "I'll come back for it again"?' asked the garda incredulously. 'You're in the film business. You should be good at making up things better than this. That description wouldn't hack it on Postman Pat.'

The interviews continued through the night. Lillis stuck desperately to his story no matter how many times it was challenged. He repeated his account of the burglar, or simply replied 'no comment'. He could not be shaken or moved. Finally, at 7.15 in the morning, Eamonn Lillis was charged with the murder of his wife.

CHAPTER 5

A Remarkable Life Remembered

Lillis appeared in Cloverhill district court the next day, to be formally charged with his wife's murder. He looked rough after the twenty-four hours of questioning and appeared in the court looking wan and drawn, wearing a pale grey hoodie top and blue jeans. Throughout the brief proceedings he clutched a book tightly, speaking only once when the charge was read out to him. He replied:

'Nothing to say.'

Lillis was remanded in custody to appear again the following morning. He would still be in custody two days later, on the day of his wife's funeral, and would remain on remand until the new year.

The tributes to Celine had been pouring in since news of her death was made public the previous week. People in the advertising and film communities were lining up to pay their respects to the woman who so many had worked with and whose achievements in her field were well known and respected. Flocking to specialist online forums, those who had known her shared their shock and grief. She might have sometimes rubbed people up the wrong way but people now talked about the 'tough and feisty producer' with awe and affection. It was widely acknowledged that while she was a tough businesswoman she was also generous. It was commented that she would 'always stop to talk to you' and those that knew her voiced their concern for her only child, now suddenly facing a Christmas without either parent.

The website of the Irish Film and Television Network (IFTN) posted a tribute to her, with comments from those who had worked closely with her. Keith Hutchinson, of fellow Windmill Lane tenants H2 Films, wrote:

'It is with a very heavy and sad heart that I find myself writing a tribute to a friend and colleague, so cruelly, and

all too soon, stolen from this world. Celine was the 'Mother' of Commercial Production in Ireland. Her contribution to the industry is unparalleled. Throughout her entire career she was at the forefront of the business, constantly producing great work, nurturing talent and leading by example. The industry has lost one of its leading lights, and she will be greatly missed.

'On a more personal note, I was always amazed by Celine's kindness of spirit. Always the first with words of congratulations, or the first to send a gift for a newborn child or a wedding. It's this kind of thoughtfulness for others that is a true reflection of the person that was Celine. Her presence will be missed, but her true kindness will never be forgotten. God bless you Celine.'

Paul Brady, writing on behalf of Windmill Lane, echoed his comments. He recollected Celine's early days starting out in the studios, long before Toytown Films came into being:

'For more than 20 years Celine was a great client and true friend to Windmill Lane. In fact she got her first break into this industry when she worked on reception here but

was very quickly poached by a production company client who spotted her true potential. After a number of years gaining experience in the production sector she took the opportunity to set up her own company Toytown Films which she ran with great enthusiasm and passion. Coming full circle, Celine came back to where she started her career and chose to base her successful company, Toytown Films in Windmill Lane. Sadly, we now all miss her vibrant presence and would like to extend our sincere sympathy to her family, friends and work colleagues.'

Those who knew her outside the cutthroat world of film also sent their sympathies to the family of the woman they had known so well. Producer John McDonnell, who was a close friend of Celine's as well as a colleague, wrote most movingly on the IFTN tribute page:

'Sitting here writing about Celine ... I still can't believe that she is gone. She had a huge influence on me throughout my career on a professional level but more importantly on a personal level, supportive and encouraging when it came to family. She was always available with words of wisdom and comfort as you deal with the many

obstacles that life throws at you. We worked together for many years and we referred to her affectionately as "Mum". She was a unique person with a heart of gold. I will miss her. My thoughts are with her family, many friends and colleagues.'

Tennis star John McEnroe recalled the girl who had once gone out with his kid brother.

'They seemed like a good pair. My heart goes out to her parents, one of whom I saw recently in Belfast, and her daughter. What a senseless tragedy.'

The media were in a frenzy. This was the most high profile killing that had come their way in a long time. With Celine's connections to the film and modelling worlds and her family's connections to the country's political elite, the case had a genuine air of celebrity to it. The papers approached as many high profile names as they could. Broadcaster Gay Byrne told the *Evening Herald* that he had seen the Cawley family out walking their dogs when he and his family lived in Howth. His daughter, Crona, he said had been of an age with Celine and had known her well.

'Of course she is completely shocked and horrified to hear about what happened and how Celine died. It's terrible for the family because one of the other daughters died a few years ago from a terminal illness.'

Even Roger Moore himself, who had starred as James Bond in Celine's one foray into acting, was asked for his opinion of her death when he visited Dublin to promote his autobiography, *My Word is My Bond*. He told the eager press:

'I remember Celine well – she was a lovely woman. I heard the news and I was sorry for her. It was a real tragedy.'

By the time Celine's funeral was to take place, on Christmas Eve, the excitement had grown to fever pitch. The crowds that gathered outside the Church of the Assumption in Howth spilled out onto the street and the journalists attended in droves. The church was already full several hours before the ceremony was due to start. The altar was covered in a simple purple cloth, embroidered with the single word 'Love'. A huge Christmas tree stood in the corner of the church, a jarringly festive note in the grief-stricken proceedings. In the absence of Lillis, who, as the service began was being further remanded in custody to spend Christmas at Cloverhill Prison until a bail of €75,000 could be produced, his daughter was left to be the chief mourner at her mother's funeral. She presented, a pale, hollow-eyed figure in the throngs outside the church. All the great and the good were there. Not only those who had known and loved Celine but those there to support her family, in particular her father James, forced to mark the passing of another loved one a little over a year after he had buried his beloved wife Brenda. The acute pain he was suffering was deeply etched on his face and the emotion he was feeling could be clearly seen in his eyes.

At 12.10 the sleek black hearse arrived with Celine's coffin. The strong young voices of the choir from Celine's daughter's school lifted in a heartfelt rendition of Take That's 'Rule the World' as the light oak coffin made its slow progress to the heart of the church. The girl followed her mother's coffin down the aisle before taking her seat with the rest of her family in the front row of pews. It was a family friend, Fr Ciaran O'Carroll, who led the service. In his homily he described Celine's death as a heartbreaking experience:

'The loss of someone who is so loved, the death of someone to whom we feel so close and to whom we owe so much, is indeed an incredibly painful, distressing and heartbreaking experience.' He added:

'The death of someone so bright, so full of light and promise, makes us somehow look at life in a different way.'

He commented that Celine had so tragically lost her life close to the winter solstice, the darkest, bleakest time of the year, and for her family there had been nothing but dark nights since she had died. He described Celine as 'a do-er, with a flair and an ability to get things done with panache and style.' He said she was an honest and loyal woman with a dramatic and passionate nature.

'We cherish the memory of someone who was incredibly young, kind, thoughtful and considerate.'

During the offertory, as the gifts were brought to the altar, the school choir once more lifted their voices to sing the haunting harmonies of the Christmas hymn 'Oh

Holy Night'. Speaking on behalf of the family, Andrew Coonan, husband of Celine's sister, Susanna, described the family's loss as 'appalling'. He thanked the crowds for coming to show their support to the Cawley family, and said:

'It is the time ahead, the months ahead, the years ahead, that we will need your support more so.'

Outside the church, as the crowds poured out into the grey winter day, the mourners were met by a small crowd of photographers, waiting to get shots of the family's tears as the coffin was loaded back into the hearse for its final journey to the crematorium at Glasnevin Cemetery. The family clung together, watching the coffin push through the crowds. A stream of political heavyweights queued to pay their respects to James Cawley. Maureen Haughey, the widow of the former taoiseach, was there with her children Sean, Eimear and Ciaran, as were politicians Michael Woods, Terence Flanagan and Ivor Callely. Senator Feargal Quinn and Justice Ronan Keane also took a moment to convey their condolences to the family. In the midst of all the crowds and general crush, Celine's seventeen-year-old daughter looked on. Photographs taken that day show a flash of her mother's spirit in the look she gave the photographers pressing against the gates of the church. Her expression reflects the same anguish expressed by her aunt Susanna thirteen months later at Lillis's sentencing. In her victim impact statement, Susanna would say that the funeral had descended into a media circus, 'bereft of the usual ritual and comfort'.

After they had seen Celine to her final resting place, the family fled the curious, sympathetic stares to spend what was left of the Christmas season in Austria. In Cloverhill Prison, Lillis spent a very lonely Christmas on remand. Finally, on 30 December, he was granted bail. The amount had been set at €75,000, with an additional €75,000 should he ever abscond and a further independent surety of €50,000. His old college friend and former advertising colleague, Gerry Kennedy, agreed to go guarantor by providing the surety. But it was not until 6 January that Lillis could secure the money in the bustle of the Christmas season. He was finally released and went home to Rowan Hill, the house now empty and quiet, his wife's blood washed away from the wooden planks of the decking where she had lain dying. Lillis settled back into his former life as much as he could. Although he had not changed his story of the masked intruder as far as the authorities were concerned, he now felt the urge to come clean to his daughter. For the first time he described the row that had started on that morning and how it had built to a tragic conclusion.

He had also decided to tell Jean Treacy, but it was some months before he managed to speak his former lover. He met with her several more times and even dropped letters into her new workplace. But Jean no longer wanted his attention. When he twice dropped mail into the salon where she had gone to work after her sudden departure from the Howth Haven and she also saw him in his car near the house where she lived with her fiancé Keith, Ms Treacy had had enough. Since Celine had died, their passion had cooled and she was now trying to pick up the pieces of her life that had been so suddenly shattered that morning. She took his final lavish gift, a diamond Tiffany pendant, straight to the gardaí and related to them the story he had told her about his wife's death.

In June 2009 Eamonn Lillis was brought back to court to be reminded that talking to the woman who was now one of the prosecution's chief witnesses against him was not an option. Dressed in a smart charcoal grey suit with a white shirt and navy tie, close to the outfit he would wear every day of his trial the following year, Lillis stared straight ahead as he was told not to have any further contact with Jean Treacy, his face revealing no emotion whatsoever. The old wood panelled room in Court 1 in the historic Four Courts building was surprisingly busy on the Thursday of an otherwise quiet week. Even for such a small bit of legal business, Eamonn Lillis was already a name that could ensure a substantial crowd of journalists. There was not much to be said about the brief appearance, lasting less than five minutes, but the assembled press were careful to note down every detail.

Looking around the courtroom, Lillis's barrister, Roisin Lacey, told Mr Justice Paul Carney that the defence were already concerned about the level of media attention the case was getting and would like the court to make a note of the fact. Mr Justice Carney nodded his assent and the brief matter was concluded. As Lillis got up and left the court, text messages were quickly sent from the assembled press to alert the photographers outside, who would have to wait until he exited the building before they could get their shot. It would be their last chance until the trial began the following January.

For the next few months Lillis faded from the public consciousness. Now that he had been charged, the press could no longer pick over the details of the case for fear of prejudicing the trial. No paper wanted to be the one that got the trial postponed or even collapsed the case if the defence succeeded in proving that a fair trial was impossible after so much media scrutiny. As 2009 drew to an end, economic news dominated the papers as Ireland watched the riches of the Celtic Tiger economy dwindle and slip away. The anniversary of Celine's death came and went unmarked by the media but keenly felt by her family. They would have to wait until the new court term started for a resolution to the legal limbo they found themselves in. Lillis continued his life in the shadow of the trial. In April 2009 he wound up Toytown Films. The company, although still highly profitable, had been damaged by what had happened. In a business where image mattered so much, the violent death of its founder and the accusation of her partner was a fairly insurmountable problem. Much would be made of this move after his conviction, but for the next few months it went largely unremarked. The press were biding their time until the trial opened in January. This was truly going be the biggest trial of the new century.

CHAPTER 6

The Trial of the Decade

The trial began on 11 January 2010, almost thirteen months after that frosty morning in 2008. There was still snow on the ground after the coldest Christmas in over forty years, but it didn't stop the crowds coming for a look. That Monday morning, the photographers gathered outside the newly built Criminal Courts of Justice on Parkgate Street in Dublin. Lillis was to have the distinction of being the first man accused of a high profile killing to stand trial in the new courts rather than in the historic Four Courts complex. The building was the subject of much discussion as the journalists filed into the long wooden benches and waited impatiently for the jury selection to start. A shiny fortress of glass and steel, it was a stark contrast to the worn stone and polished wood of the James Gandon designed Round Hall in the Four Courts.

Lillis sat stiffly in the small enclosure set aside for the accused. There is no dock in an Irish court, so despite the rather caged look, it was simply a seat. Wearing an austere black suit with a crisp white shirt and dark tie, Lillis's face showed the stress of anticipation. As the court filled up, he frequently gestured impatiently for his solicitor to come over to him and clarify some small matter. Each time, he lifted his hand and beckoned with one finger raised. He didn't glance towards the rows of press sitting only a couple of feet in front of him. Neither did his eyes flick towards his wife's family, sitting tensely at the back of the courtroom, or even towards his two sisters, Elaine and Carmel, who had made the trip over from their homes in England to be with him as he faced trial.

Finally, a few minutes after the set time, the Central Criminal Court's top judge took his seat. Mr Justice Paul Carney is a well known and sometimes controversial figure, but today his job was simply to oversee the swearing in of the jury. The trial itself would be handled by another judge. The entire courtroom rose as he took his seat, then settled back into expectant silence, waiting for the selection process to begin. The registrar got to her feet behind the barricade of computer screens and printers that marked her seat in the bench below the judge. From a wooden box in front of her she drew a handful of cardboard rectangles and began to read out a list of names. After a few seconds, a parade of men and women started to emerge from the door at the back of the spacious jury box. They stood uncertainly, looking out into the busy body of the court. As if to put them at their ease, Judge Carney explained the process. The selected names would be read out again and both prosecution and defence had the option to refuse up to seven potential jurors. He said that they weren't to take it seriously if this happened. It could be for any reason – that they were wearing a tie, or maybe that they weren't – nobody would ever know. The registrar glanced up at him again, then began to read through the list of names. At each name, one of the jury panel stepped forward in the expectation of filling one of the twelve seats. There was a brief pause as they waited for any objection, then they would take the little blue-covered New Testament from the desk in front of them and repeat the oath read out to them. Some of them repeated the words confidently, almost with a swagger; others stumbled and whispered so quietly that they couldn't be heard above the quiet rustling of the attentive courtroom. The room was silent as each of them promised to listen to the evidence and decide the verdict according to the facts of the case presented to them in court.

Lillis watched each face intently as if trying to read the person's entire life story. He had no more information than the little allowed to prosecution and defence: the names and occupations of those in front of them. But he was very definite in his conclusions. As soon as someone he didn't approve of stood forward he would start shaking his head, his head bent towards that of his solicitor who was standing against the outside of the dockless box, leaning over his client. The potential jurors that Lillis discarded with such finality were all women. Any woman who looked comfortably middle-aged, or whose hair had been able to follow its natural inclination was dismissed with a peremptory shake of the head. Puffa jackets were out, as were the women who, it seemed, didn't come up to his sartorial standards. The five women who eventually took their seats were similar in one very clear respect. They all looked middle class.

The prosecution had their own ideas about who would fit in the jury. They refused the younger men, the obvious students, or those who looked as if their career might not have been fully mapped out for them. In the end it was the prosecution who refused the male panel members who failed to meet whatever mysterious criteria were in place. Eventually, a jury of seven men and five women were sitting in the two rows of seats. The registrar read through the names again, checking the order of those selected. Judge Carney looked down on them and delivered his customary warning. It was their 'last chance saloon,' he said, meaning that if there were likely to be any problems, now was the time to speak up. For example, were they all able to stay with the trial until its conclusion, which might be three weeks away? Immediately several hands shot up. There was a soft groan from the press bench as the nervous few were excused and the registrar stood up to pick another handful of cards from the wooden box. The second batch of jurors arrived and the selection worked as it had before. Finally, six men and six women sat and promised that they would be able to stick with it until the end, whenever that might be. Lillis's defence counsel, Brendan Grehan SC, stood up as soon as they had finished, to tell the court that if matters could be postponed until the following day, proceedings would be able to be simplified considerably. Judge Carney nodded and informed the jury that the trial would start the following morning at 11 o'clock. As the jury filed out, there was an exodus from the courtroom as several dozen journalists rushed to file the first titbit of news.

The next morning, the photographers were waiting outside the courts again as Lillis arrived with his sisters. The trial was to take place on the sixth floor of the new building, and by 10.30 a crowd had already gathered. There was a problem with passes into the new court-rooms and Lillis and his legal team had to wait until a member of court staff bustled up with the appropriate swipe card to allow them into one of the consultation rooms for their morning conference. Lillis stood as far away from the crowd as possible, turned away from the curious stares, as if looking out over Dublin Bay rather than the central well of the courts building.

Proceedings eventually commenced a little after the appointed time when the trial judge, Mr Justice Barry White, took his seat. He was no stranger to this level of public interest, having already overseen the trials of Joe O'Reilly and Brian Kearney, both men convicted of killing their wives and whose cases had been tried in the full glare of the media spotlight.

Once the jury had taken their seats, Mary Ellen Ring SC opened the case for the prosecution. A charismatic figure with a shock of pure white wavy hair to her shoulders, contrasting with the severity of her black barrister's gown, she ran through the final hours of Celine Cawley's life. A ripple of interest passed round the court as she told the jury that they would be hearing the details of Lillis's affair with his masseuse, Jean Treacy. She touched on the forensic evidence and told the jury about the discovery of the Rip Curl suitcase in the attic, but the longest

time was spent itemising the complex lies she alleged Lillis had told in the days following his wife's death. Lillis gazed straight ahead of him, avoiding the eyes of the jury members, as the details of the investigation were summarised. He didn't react as Ms Ring painted the case against him in the blackest of black tones and, if he was nervous now that the trial had finally started, it barely showed.

Ms Ring finished putting forward her case and the first witnesses were ready to be called, but before she could summon them, Brendan Grehan got to his feet. Lillis glanced quickly at his barrister in anticipation of what was about to happen. A master at commanding attention, Brendan Grehan was one of Ireland's most renowned criminal defence counsels. He had appeared for a litany of high profile defendants, including Padraig Nally, Linda Mulhall and Ronnie Dunbar. With him fighting their corner, Nally was acquitted of the manslaughter of traveller John 'Frog' Ward. Dunbar, accused of the murder and seduction of Sligo teenager Melissa Mahon, was finally convicted of manslaughter, as was Mulhall, one of the two so-called Scissor Sisters who had killed and dismembered their mother's boyfriend, Farah Swaleh Noor. Now, once again, Mr Grehan was apparently facing improbable odds. The case Ms Ring had outlined had contained damning forensics, sexual intrigue and lies, but in moments Mr Grehan had scored his first direct hit on the prosecution case with a series of admissions that rendered useless the carefully constructed series of proofs they had been planning to use to unmask Lillis's assailant as the phantom it really was.

After a list of fairly standard defence admissions – that the gardaí had conducted their investigation properly and that Lillis's human rights had not been encroached upon during his detention, Mr Grehan dropped a bombshell that caused every journalist's pen to start spiking like a needle on a lie detector machine. They carefully took down every word as he informed the court that his client, Eamonn Lillis, admitted there was no burglar in the house that morning. There was 'no burglar in the home, no intruder or other party present other than the accused himself on the occasion when Celine Cawley suffered the injuries that resulted in her death.'

Surprising as such an admission was, it didn't pause the proceedings and the jury were immediately immersed in explanations of dozens of crime scene photographs taken by gardaí in the hours after the drama, showing the bloody scene where Celine had lain dying. The new courthouse offered state of the art technological possibilities as far as this kind of evidence was concerned and the Office of the Director of Public Prosecutions was making full use of them. Each one of the several dozen photographs handed to the jury and counsel in red-covered, spiral bound booklets was also shown on the large screens that hung on either side of the wall behind Justice White, and also on the wall facing the jury, behind the accused.

The public who were crushed into the back of the courtroom leaned forward to see the pool of blood on the decking. They saw gardaí standing by the covered outdoor hot tub, pointing at the incriminating blood spatter on the pebble-dashed wall. The ornamental cow was pointed out beside a gap in the hedge where the fictional attacker had been supposed to have made his escape.

For many who didn't have the benefit of newspaper archives it was the first time they had glimpsed the leafy affluence of Windgap Road, and before the photographs were finished, the attraction of the trial was cemented.

After lunch, the crowd was even bigger to hear Lillis's panicked voice echo across the courtroom as the recording of his 999 call was played, in a brief respite to the succession of ambulance drivers and gardaí who had reconstructed the agreed facts of the morning of 15 December. The pool of blood on the decking was flashed on the screens again and again as witness after witness described arriving at the scene. Lillis's demeanour was analysed in triplicate and the first accounts of his lies were given. Celine's family sat quietly through the evidence, showing a dignified, united front. Lillis gazed at the screens each time the scene of his wife's death was shown, but his face stayed impassive, as it would throughout most of the trial.

He didn't even react the following day when the prosecution introduced a superlative opportunity for Grade A rubber-necking with a DVD tour of the crime scene. This wouldn't be the first time a jury had been shown around the scene of the crime. While it's not a standard part of the prosecution case, there have been numerous occasions in the past when juries have been bussed to a disputed scene, along with the judge and court staff. Up until the opening of the new Criminal Courts of Justice, a bus trip was the usual method of coming to terms with the three dimensional layout of the scene of a crime. But the gardaí investigating Celine Cawley's death had imagined other opportunities. On 21 December, while Lillis was being interrogated about the death of his wife, gardaí had taken a video camera on a tour of Rowan Hill. It was this footage that was shown to the court. There was a hush as the film started. There was no audio; the detective sergeant whose footsteps we were tracing gave a live running commentary as the camera swept through the house.

Almost immediately it was apparent that this was an unprecedented tour. The restless gaze of the camera swept over the decking, pausing on the hot tub before turning to look over the rolling lawn. The daisy-patterned ornamental cow was treated to the full cinematic zoom and the terracotta menagerie that dotted the garden were each given a featured roll. Inside the house, after pausing to sweep over the blood spatter on the pebble-dash, each strand of tinsel was scrutinised and passed by. The moving image gave a far more emotional impression than the more clinical still photographs. Breakfast things left out on the kitchen counter, the Christmas tree standing forlorn in a corner of the sitting room with an empty dog bed in front of it, everything had a newly abandoned feel. The camera wandered away from the crime scene into the rest of the house, speeding up briefly in the interests of privacy to whisk backwards and forwards through the empty room of the beloved only child. At the end of a hallway it turned into the bedroom Celine had woken in on her last morning, stopping to examine the jars and bottles on the bathroom shelves. Then it was off upstairs. At the top of the stairs the attic door was open so the camera peered inside, its gaze passing over the boxes of children's toys and a dehumidifier box. Finally the film arrived in Lillis's master bedroom, stopping to show the view from the balcony. The impersonal glance travelled across the rumpled bed sheets and paused to examine the clutter on the dressing table: the contents of a pocket, a jumble of coins and a €10 note. Then, with one last peek out of the window, the film ended.

There was silence in the courtroom as people processed what they had just seen. Justice White quietly asked the jury to leave the court. He sat in silence until the last one had left, then turned angrily to prosecution junior counsel Paul Greene. What additional benefit had that film been, he wanted to know.

'What has it done other than appease the gruesome appetite of some members of the public to see the home? I ask that the Director of Public Prosecutions considers putting forward relevant evidence rather than putting on a show trial.'

Paul Greene stood his ground. The prosecution had selected the evidence of the greatest possible assistance to the jury, he said. They had wanted to make full use of the new facilities to give the best possible view of the home.

A young Celine Cawley

Left: Celine Cawley during her modelling days

Below: Celine with Jack Charlton in Kinsale, Co. Cork in September 1990.

Above: 17th August 1984. Roger Moore (James Bond) and the 'Bond Girls' pictured during the shooting of 'A View to a Kill'. Celine Cawley is on the left in the back row, immediately in front of the flower arrangement. (Courtesy of The Sunday Independent)

Below: Juliet Hussey (left) with her cousin Celine Cawley.

Left: The gatepost at Rowan Hill, the Lillis-Cawley home.

Below: The patio to the rear of Rowan Hill, where Celine Cawley died.

Photos: Michael Stamp

Right: Jean Treacy

Below: Howth Haven Beauty Clinic, where Jean Teacy first met Eamonn Lillis.

Above: The remains of Celine Cawley are carried from the Church of The Assumption in Howth after her funeral Mass.

Below: Ombudsman Emily O'Reilly offers her condolences to James Cawley, father of Celine Cawley.

Right: Susanna Cawley accompanies her father, James, to the Court.

Collins Photo Agency

Below (left to right): Andrew Coonan, husband of Susanna Cawley, Sorcha Cawley and her husband, Chris Cawley, Celine's brother, outside the Criminal Courts of Justice.

Photo © The Sunday Independent

Above: Celine Cawley's brother, Chris, delivers his statement to the media after the sentencing.

Below: Eamonn Lillis outside the Criminal Courts of Justice, Dublin.

Justice White was not impressed. What did the bedroom and bathroom of the deceased have to do with the prosecution's account of what had happened that day? And what possible evidential value could there be in showing the teenage daughter's bedroom and recreation room?

'It reminds me of the show trial that was put on in America not many years ago, the O J Simpson trial.'

His opinion given, he called for the jury to come back in and the trial resumed. The crowd chattered quietly among themselves. After the tedium of the morning's evidence so far, even with the high tech frills, the spat had been the first bit of genuine drama of the trial. But the video was the thing that tipped the public interest. Once the colour writers had run through the full details of the virtual tour for the following morning's papers the crowds increased even further. They started arriving at court in their dozens. Each morning the attendance grew larger. By the end of the first week, the throng was six deep at the back of the court and the overflow spilled right out into the corridor outside. They were coming from all over Dublin, all over Ireland. Some were friends, neighbours, acquaintances of Celine Cawley and Lillis himself. Others were the regular faces who come to observe every day of every major murder trial. More had found their way to the court simply because it was the biggest news story of the day that had seating for members of the public. Some appeared to treat the proceedings as entertainment, bringing a packed lunch and delighting in any longer lunch break caused by a legal hiccup because they could now get their errands done and be back in time to make 'the afternoon show'. One man was there because his holiday flight had been cancelled in a strike at Dublin Airport and he wanted something else to do.

Every morning, Lillis would arrive with his sisters and one of the close friends who had stood by him throughout the investigation and stand to one side. When his legal team arrived and the door was opened to get into the consultation room, the crowd would part like a sea, leaving barely enough space for him to pass. As he pushed his way through, they would press forward and hands would reach out as if he were a celebrity sur-rounded by a crush of fans.

On the Wednesday of the second week the crowd peaked. A sixth sense must have drawn them, as today would turn out to be the day the most anticipated witness was to take the stand. Great secrecy had surrounded the attendance of Lillis's former mistress, and gardaí would not even tell the press what day she was due to appear. As the press were allowed in to take their seats it became apparent that there were more gardaí than usual, stand-ing in a close group in the back left hand corner of the room, where witnesses were usually seated. A trim figure sat on the bench behind them, sipping water out of a bottle through a straw. In his enclosure Lillis avoided even a glance in that direction, but as he bent over the pages in front of him he blinked his eyes rapidly as the unfamiliar contact lenses irritated his corneas. The fact that he had been willing to put up with this obvious dis-comfort in place of his usual glasses was commented upon gleefully in the press benches. It appeared that a conscious attempt had been made to look his best when his former mistress took the stand. Two full benches of journalists were in attendance, not to mention three sketch artists, eager to get every witness box expression down in charcoal for posterity. The public surged in, massing behind the back row, where the Cawley family sat as usual. Today was going to be something special – even those who had never set foot in a court could tell that the ring of gardaí around the seated figure in the corner could only mean something good.

Before the masseuse could take the stand, however, another witness had to be dealt with. It appeared that the gardaí had taken the unprecedented step of bringing two civilian witnesses, who had nothing more than embarrassment to fear, into court with the kind of protection normally reserved for the witnesses of gangland crimes. Before the judge had taken his seat, the texts started arriving from the photographers waiting in the cold outside. Where was Jean Treacy? She hadn't been past them. Neither had neighbour Pauline Fraser, who took to the witness stand briefly to describe hearing a high-pitched scream on the morning Celine died. She sat stiffly as she was questioned, hardly moving her jaw to answer, obviously acutely embarrassed at such a public interrogation. Her evidence was fast, but it wasn't Ms Fraser's words that people were craning to hear that morning. It was to get a better view of the slim brunette sitting behind her wall of gardaí, sipping away at her water.

Eventually Ms Treacy took the stand. Dressed in black trousers and a white shirt, a knee length black cardigan belted around her waist, her hair sleek and highlighted, she looked groomed and composed. Every eye followed her as she made her way to the front of the stand to take her seat … every eye except for that of her former lover. Lillis kept his eyes turned towards his notes, but his face reddened as she passed. Jean Treacy took her seat and sat waiting for questions. There was no way she was going to come out of this looking good. The court had already heard technical phone evidence that had itemised the passionate affair, stripping it down to bare statistics. Phone evidence had revealed that communication between the lovers had peaked in the fortnight before Celine Cawley met her violent death. In those two weeks they had exchanged over 200 text messages and called each other more than a hundred times. The details of the texts she had kept on her phone had been read out in court, so everyone watching knew that she had told Lillis 'I love you infinitely' and finished her texts with an X, representing a kiss. As she took the stand that morning there was already much speculation about the contents of the two 'multi-media' messages she had sent him. The perception of her was very much that of a 'scarlet woman', but as she sat down she looked like butter wouldn't melt in her mouth.

She quickly ran through the route that had brought her into contact with Lillis, the night courses while she was still working in marketing, getting a job in the Howth Haven Beauty Clinic in August 2006. She explained how it had been Celine who had first been her client, coming to her for deep tissue massage. Celine hadn't liked to be massaged too hard, Ms Treacy told the court: 'She really didn't like too much pain.' Flicking her hair, she described how Ms Cawley had introduced her husband when he was suffering from back pain. He had also come to her for deep tissue massage, she said.

Ms Ring guided her gently through the account of the affair, keeping carefully to the less embarrassing details. Ms Treacy agreed that her relationship with Lillis had changed after he had invited her to come out and see photographs of his dogs that were saved on his iPod. She described noticing Lillis's hands as he scrolled through the pictures on his iPod. 'They were just particularly nice for a man's hands.' She did not blush as she described the moment she put his hand on her pulse so he could feel her beating heart. 'This is what I'm feeling,' she quoted. Quite what she and Lillis had got up to in the throes of passion was quickly glossed over. She acknowledged that it was an 'intimate, sexual' relationship but didn't mention any trysts in the salon or clandestine meetings in the back of Lillis's car in shopping centre car parks. The affair as it was described in court sounded almost chaste. Ms Treacy tilted her chin, her voice taking an upward inflection at the end of the more awkward answers. She had known that Lillis's marriage was unhappy, she said, but there was never any talk of him leaving his wife. She had merely been caught up in the throes of passion. Had she developed feelings for Lillis, Ms Ring wanted to know. For the only time while she was in court, Jean Treacy's eyes darted towards the man to her right, sitting with his head bowed. 'At the time I thought I had, but I realise now it was more of an infatuation.'

Lillis did not look up.

Ms Treacy continued quickly. She described how she and Lillis had arranged to meet on 15 December. She had asked him to bring the Mercedes ML jeep because it was more comfortable and the blacked out windows meant you weren't looking over your shoulder all the time. 'Not from a seedy or sordid point of view,' she hastened to add. There was just more legroom. She was quickly led away from dangerous liaisons and back to the matter at hand. She told the court that she had texted Lillis several times on the morning his wife died but had got no reply. She only got to talk to him late that night when he finally answered his phone. She was, at that stage, '100% convinced' that his story of a burglary was true. Once again, the text messages were reprised. Ms Treacy agreed that she had sent Lillis a message offering her support in such a difficult time and telling him she would see him at his wife's funeral.

James Cawley sat at the back of the courtroom, his face pale and stiff as he finally saw the woman with whom Lillis had been cheating on his daughter. Ms Treacy didn't look at him. She kept her eyes firmly fixed on Ms Ring as she answered the questions and navigated her way through her story of betrayal. She didn't look at her former lover as she described the distinct cooling off that had happened between them in the days after Celine's death. He had been due to attend his massage appointment the Friday following Celine's death, but Howth Haven cancelled on behalf of their errant employee. She had her own worries, she explained. It had become necessary to take leave from her job in the days that followed. She didn't say whether this decision had been left for her to take or forced upon her, but her economy with words only underlined how much her infatuation had cost her. By the time Lillis was arrested she had lost her job and her summer wedding was in serious jeopardy.

She explained that she hadn't spoken to Lillis again until after he was released from the mandatory period of incarceration that follows a murder charge.

The questioning moved on to their next meeting. Ms Treacy said that Lillis had started to call her twenty-four hours after he was released from prison on 6 January. He left several voice messages asking her to call him, but she didn't respond. The following day he arrived at her house. He didn't stop or get out of his car, just made a U-turn in the drive. She hadn't actually spoken to him until March 2009 when he had insisted on telling her a radically different version of what had taken place on that morning in December to the account he had so far given to the police and Celine's family. She tilted her chin up as she explained 'I originally said I didn't want to know anything about it but he insisted on telling me. He said he felt he owed me an explanation.'

She set out Lillis's account as he had told it to her. That he had forgotten to take out the rubbish and Celine had just gone mad. She looked straight ahead and spoke distinctly as she went on: 'She started hurling abuse, said he was a terrible husband and just useless.' The row had degenerated, she said. They both said things that were 'just disgusting' to each other. 'They just lost it with each other.' Celine had come out of the kitchen and slipped on the icy patio, she said, but had got straight back up. 'He made an analogy to a beach ball.' Ms Treacy said that in the scuffle that followed Lillis had held his wife up to the glass and then they had both slipped. Celine just 'went mad' and then 'all of a sudden she started biting his finger. She wouldn't let go. He just felt she was trying to bite it off.' Jean Treacy raised her hand to demonstrate how Lillis had described using his open hand to push his wife's head away from the hand that she was biting. He had pushed her 'gently', she said, but 'all of a sudden a pool of blood appeared under her head and Celine slipped out of consciousness.' There must have been a brick under her head, Ms Treacy guessed, and that was what had caused the blood. She said that Celine had come round once and had discussed with Lillis what to do. This was when the robbery plan had been agreed. 'It was the only way they could describe the physical damage, I suppose.' She said Lillis told her that Celine had slipped in and out of consciousness for a while before finally she would not wake up. Lillis said that he had immediately called 999. He told her that he had to make it look like a robbery for the sake of his daughter, 'which didn't make sense to me,' she added.

Ms Ring wanted to know if Lillis had grieved for his wife.

'He said he did. He wasn't overcome with grief, but he said he often found himself with the light on in her room and lying on her bed and he would find himself going to talk to her and realise she wasn't there.'

The explanation he had given her was almost the last time she saw Lillis before coming face to face with him in court. She had seen him once more after his account of his wife's death, but had then cut ties. He had tried to phone her a couple of times but she hadn't returned his calls. Then, on 26 May, she arrived in work to find a three-page letter from him waiting for her. With the letter was a package, wrapped in paper that was printed with the lyrics from the Beyoncé song 'Halo' and finished with a white ribbon. She had opened the package to find a Tiffany pendant studded with diamonds. Despite her fascination with Tiffany, she had immediately taken the pendant to the gardaí. Ms Treacy sat up straighter after Ms Ring had finished, but her ordeal wasn't over yet. It was now the turn of Brendan Grehan to go over her evidence with a fine tooth comb.

The level of expectation in the crowded room rose. Cross-examination was frequently where the most interesting details were revealed. But Mr Grehan was also treating the witness with care. His tone was a far cry from the combative demeanour he had assumed in some of his sparring contests with the judge and his opposite number, but his questions were tougher than any Ms Treacy had had to face so far. Mr Grehan reminded her that Lillis had been a married man and that she herself had been engaged to be married when the affair started. Lillis began rocking slightly in his seat, never catching her eye, as his former mistress agreed that 'I had taken to him, yes.' But Mr Grehan went on, 'You were attracted to him. In August that year you said so to a colleague.' Ms

Treacy didn't reply as he put it to her that she had made suggestive comments about what she would like to do to Lillis to her colleagues. She agreed that the affair had been a passionate one. Her glance flicked towards Lillis as she acknowledged that they had been to Rowan Hill together on a number of occasions. The relationship was suddenly sounding a lot seedier. Mr Grehan reminded her that Lillis had got her a phone to use for the affair after there was 'some kind of an issue with someone you knew and a contact with Mr Lillis'. 'He insisted on getting it,' she replied, obviously stung by the suggestion. She had been going to get a new phone anyway.

Mr Grehan quickly moved away from the sexual transgressions and concentrated instead on his client's personality. Ms Treacy readily agreed that her former lover was 'refined and gentle, a bit of a dreamer', and that she had thought he was someone who 'wouldn't hurt a fly'. But the respite was short-lived and the barrister was soon back to the details of the affair. He ran through the texts, highlighting the extramarital habit of the blank text checking that the coast was clear. She answered abruptly, having already gone through the details of the text traffic with Ms Ring. Mr Grehan turned to her dealings with gardaí. Why hadn't she come forward herself after Celine was killed? It had been a colleague who had given gardaí her name. Ms Treacy responded defiantly:

'It doesn't make a difference. They contacted me.'

Sensing her resistance, Mr Grehan quickly moved on to something a little less divisive. Had she been in Lillis's company when Celine had called and wanted him to come home? Relieved, she nodded quickly. They had been in the Mercedes jeep when Celine had called and asked Lillis to return with the car immediately so she could take their daughter out. 'It wasn't even what she said. She spoke to him quite badly.' Lillis hadn't reacted, she said. 'He spoke back normally,' but had seemed embarrassed.

Mr Grehan led her back to her meeting with Lillis after his release from prison. She had called him to arrange it, he suggested. She'd made the call late at night after she had been drinking. 'I had a good few drinks on me, yes.' Mr Grehan let her continue.

'It's not that I exactly wanted to ask him what happened,' she explained to the jury. 'I couldn't understand how I had got it so wrong. I just wanted to see could I get a sense of him. Had everyone else seen it? I was needing to get closure. I wanted to get a sense but didn't want to ask him straight out. More than anything else, I wanted to find out what happened.'

Why hadn't she gone straight to the gardaí with the story Lillis had told her? Why had she waited for two months to give a statement? It was because he had been following her, she said. The Tiffany pendant had not been the first thing he sent her.

'I thought, with the lack of contact, he would get the idea I didn't want anything to do with him, and only when he became problematic I went to the gardaí.' She hadn't wanted him to tell her all the details of what had happened with Celine. 'I was uncomfortable hearing it. He insisted on telling me.'

Mr Grehan tried to clear up some of the discrepancies between her account of what Lillis had told her and the instructions that he had received from his client. Hadn't the row been about meal worms, he asked? She couldn't remember. Her recollection of what he had said was patchy, she told him.

'I do remember lying in bed that night trying to piece it together', but she had forgotten so much about what had happened. 'I was under so much pressure and just couldn't take in what had happened that I couldn't take in 100%.'

Eventually Mr Grehan let her finish. Her shoulders slumped slightly as she climbed down from the witness box. She made her way back to the corner where she was immediately surrounded again by her garda posse. She didn't glance at Lillis as she passed him, nor look towards the Cawley family, who hid their feelings about her actions behind impassive masks. Ms Ring stood up and informed the court that there were no more witnesses for the day. It had been expected that Ms Treacy's evidence would take the whole day and so no one else had been called. It was now just after 12.30. Ms Treacy had been on the stand for a little over an hour and there was much disappointment among the press benches who had expected to have more for their news editors.

The courtroom emptied slowly. Everyone wanted to get a look at the woman Lillis had been romping with in the car parks of some of Dublin's major shopping centres. But despite the best efforts of the more determined onlookers, the improvised 'wall of steel' wasn't budging for curious glances. The press didn't fare any better. The gardaí were insistent on emptying the court, foiling their attempts to loiter. They soon found themselves in the corridor outside and broke off into disgruntled groups, ostensibly checking quotes, but surreptitiously checking for Ms Treacy's exit to tip off the waiting photographers and cameramen outside. As the minutes ticked away, it became apparent that she wasn't coming out of the court. At least not through the door everyone else had come in and out by. It was known that there was a secondary network of corridors through the new court complex by which jurors and those accused or convicted could get in and out of the courtroom without being accosted. The jurors came up one way, through the odd-numbered floors not accessible by the courtroom lifts. The accused had a different route, through a door behind the witness box which led down to the cells and into an underground car park where they could be loaded into a waiting prison van, away from snapping cameras. This route was not generally designed for witnesses, but gardaí had made the decision in this case to allow Ms Treacy, as well as Pauline Fraser, to make use of its privacy.

There would be no 'walk of shame' for Ms Treacy, unlike previous mistresses, including the woman who had stood by wife killer Joe O'Reilly throughout his trial and even his imprisonment. As the realisation dawned that she was not going to make an appearance, consternation began to grow among the media. Sex sells newspapers and every one of them had editors to appease. The hunt was on. The waiting photographers moved round from the front of the building to wait for the inevitable garda van. It appeared a few minutes later and speeded up as it drove towards the small crowd of snappers. One or two photographers with luckily placed cars set off in pursuit but they were met by a road block hastily assembled up North Brunswick Street, designed to foil the paparazzi dash. Back at the courts, calls were already being made delving into Ms Treacy's private life. By the weekend her picture would be on every front page, but for the moment the sketch artists' renditions were in constant demand. If she had known the determination she had sparked by her foiling of the photographers, Ms Treacy might have decided that being 'ready for her close up' might have been the simpler course of action.

CHAPTER 7

Different Accounts

The following day it was the turn of Lillis's daughter to take the stand. Once again, the corridor outside the courtroom was crowded more than an hour before the proceedings were due to start. After the previous day's excitement, the public had turned up in their dozens, eager not to miss any more salacious revelations. The prosecution had already expressed their concerns about protecting the seventeen-year-old from the intense media scrutiny that was surrounding the trial. As she was still, legally speaking, a child, it was a more serious matter than someone who merely wanted to spare their blushes. Even though she had been named extensively when she was simply the grieving daughter at her mother's funeral, now that she was also the daughter of the man accused of murder she was required by law to have total anonymity. On the first day of the trial the press were warned not to use her name in their reports, but a few days later the prosecution suggested an even more extreme form of privacy.

On the third day of the trial, before the jury took their seats for the morning's session, Mary Ellen Ring asked Justice White to direct the media not to identify the girl in any way, including the fact that she was the daughter of Eamonn Lillis and Celine Cawley. There were several concerned minutes on the press benches as she outlined the legal basis for her request. She told the judge that the Director of Public Prosecutions would prefer that the girl be referred to as 'a seventeen-year-old female', with no reference to her relationship to the accused or the deceased.

'We have to live in the real world,' Justice White informed her.

The suggestion that an unrelated teenager was staying in the house at the time Celine Cawley died would have raised more questions than it satisfied, and was an unnecessarily draconian move. There was a collective sigh of relief from the media as the judge told the court that he had no intention of giving any such direction. Now, a week later, we were about to hear what the daughter had to say about her parents.

After he had taken his seat, Justice White looked around the packed courtroom. He reminded both counsels that he had the right to clear the court if it became necessary. Lillis's daughter would be giving her evidence from a different part of the courts complex via a video link. She would be able to see and hear whoever was asking her questions and the whole court would be able to see her on the big courtroom screens as she gave her answers. After several minutes adjusting the angle of the web cams that were to be the link so that the extent of the crowding in the court wasn't visible, the barristers and the judge removed their wigs and gowns. It was considered that a barrister was less intimidating without the black wings of his gown. The severe black jackets worn underneath were a slight improvement, and the girl, when she eventually took her seat in the little room somewhere else in the building, didn't seem unduly fazed.

Justice White introduced himself and explained that the next person who spoke to her would be the barrister for the prosecution. The girl listened carefully to what he told her and nodded abruptly. Her head and shoulders filled the three large courtroom screens. In smaller boxes, down the side of the screen, her view of her questioner could be seen, as well as a bird's eye view of the little room she was sitting in. Lillis looked up as she took her seat and his eyes remained fixed on the screen throughout her testimony, scanning every inch of his daughter's face as if reaching out to her with his thoughts. The camera in the court turned its attention to Ms Ring, who smilingly introduced herself and gently began her questioning. There was no attempt to discuss the events of 15 December, in which she had no part anyway. Ms Ring led her directly to January 2009. She had just returned from Austria, where she had been while her father was on remand in prison. Her father was released in early January.

'Did you speak to him?' Ms Ring wanted to know.

'He just told me what had happened between him and Mum. I can't exactly remember. It had just been the world's worst Christmas for me.'

The girl spoke clearly, in clipped tones, her apparent confidence an obvious mask to hide her nerves and the awful position she found herself in. Her father had given her an account of her mother's death, she said. As she laid out the rather sketchy details that she remembered, the similarities with the account Jean Treacy had given the day before were clear. The girl told the court that her parents had argued on the decking outside the kitchen.

'They had a bit of, like, a scuffle and that was it.'

Ms Ring asked her about the burglary story, and Lillis watched his daughter's face harden as she thought of her answer. Some of her confidence evaporated as she responded. The pain of the betrayal was obvious.

'He said he just panicked and he didn't know what to do, and he did it for me.' Lillis's eyes didn't leave the screen, but his daughter looked down briefly before continuing quickly.

'But I didn't really appreciate that he did it.'

She confirmed the details of the lie and then paused again.

'He asked me could I forgive him and I said yes, but I couldn't really forgive him for the lie.'

Brendan Grehan picked up the questioning as the camera turned to him. He smiled into it and introduced himself. 'I am under strict instructions to keep you here for as short a time as possible.'

The teenager laughed for the first time since she had sat down, seeming to relax slightly. He led her gently through her account of the fight again, checking details about what her father had told her.

'Do you remember him mentioning a row about meal worms for the robin or anything like that?'

'No.'

He moved on to the next point.

'Do you remember him telling you they were out on the deck and your mum slipped and hit her head on a brick? She had taken the brick with her; she had turned and hit him with the brick.'

She nodded.

'Yeah. To the best of my knowledge that's what happened.'

'They had a scuffle and your mum slipped on the decking again?' Mr Grehan repeated her earlier words back to her. 'Your dad's finger was injured.'

She nodded matter of factly.

'Yeah. It was bitten by my mum.'

The barrister pushed on.

'Did he tell you he panicked?'

'Pretty much, yeah.' She laughed nervously before continuing, suddenly serious. 'I was always brought up never to lie, so I don't really appreciate what he did for me, but I understand why he panicked to save himself.'

She repeated again that she was unable to forgive her father for his lies, and then her evidence was at an end. Her face disappeared from the three large screens and her father looked away and back down to his notes. Christopher Cawley and his wife got up and quietly left the courtroom as the teenager finished her evidence, presumably to meet her after her ordeal. Their exit went largely unnoticed. Mr Grehan leaned back in his seat, looking very happy with the morning's work.

Mary Ellen Ring stood up to say that the prosecution

case was almost over and that there would be only one more witness. Dr Michael Curtis, the assistant state pathologist, would be that final witness, but he was giving evidence in another court. Everyone was suddenly reminded that there were other trials going on in the complex, ignored as they fell outside the spotlight being shone so glaringly on the Lillis trial. Matters would have to be adjourned till after lunch, when the doctor could make an appearance.

The various accounts of the crime having been dealt with, the evidence moved into forensics. For the next couple of days Celine's family were forced to listen to the gruesome details of the investigation into her suspicious death. Post mortem evidence is some of the most difficult for the family as the person they remember is reduced to a catalogue of injuries. In her victim impact statement at the end of the trial, Celine's sister Susanna Cawley, said that the image of her sister's shaved head and bruised face had robbed her of the memory of the living person she had known and loved. Now, her family sat stiffly through the litany of scratches and scrapes given by Dr

Curtis's evidence. At the end of the trial, Susanna would talk about how the brutal post mortem description haunted them, obscuring the image of the much loved sister. Her father, in particular, appeared to find the evidence especially difficult, the pain of hearing how his child had died was etched clearly on his face.

In his customarily academic way, Dr Curtis described the woman he had found before him. He told the court that on 16 December 2008 he had started the post mortem of a middle aged woman. She was between 5'10" and 5'10½" and was markedly obese. A ring around her iris showed that she suffered from high cholesterol, and tiny pin prick haemorrhages visible in the whites of her eyes showed that lack of oxygen may have been a factor in her death. Her final struggle was attested to by the numerous scrapes on her face and bruising to her arm and thigh. There was also a bruise on her left shoulder blade that may or may not have been consistent with being pushed up against the hard metal frame of the living room window. But the main wounds were to her head. There were three of them. One towards the front, on the left side above the ear; another on the right, towards the top of the head; the third was at the back of the head to the right of the bump that forms the base of the skull. Two of the wounds were horizontal and had penetrated to the skull itself. All would have bled profusely.

He told the court that, in his opinion, the two wounds to the side of the head would not have been caused by a fall, they were too high up on the head. The one at the back could have been a fall, but the scenarios that had been given by both Jean Treacy and Lillis's daughter were unlikely. Leading him through his primary evidence, Ms Ring asked him whether it was possible that Celine had slipped, got straight back up before being pushed backwards with force against the window, then slipped again and banged her head on a brick lying on the ground. He thought for a moment before replying.

'In my opinion, that account does not in any way provide a satisfactory explanation of the injuries of the deceased.'

Dr Curtis explained that Celine had died from a combination of causes. She would have lost a lot of blood from the head wounds and her heart would have quickly become deprived of oxygen. Her weight would have meant that her lungs would not have been able to fill properly while she was lying down, and her enlarged heart, another side effect of her weight gain, had been unable to take the strain, so she would have suffocated. Slipping back into lecture room terminology, which effectively distanced the humanity from his account, he listed the official cause of death as 'blunt force trauma to the head, postural asphyxia and hypertrophic cardiomyopathy'. The phrase was left to hang in the air for a moment before matters moved on to the next stage of his evidence – the analysis of what had caused the injuries, and through them, the death.

Dr Curtis had been back to Rowan Hill a second time, after Lillis had been arrested and Celine had been buried. In January 2009 he had gone with gardaí to examine the decking area where Celine had died. The pool of blood where she had lain was long since washed away, but he had wanted to examine the texture of the wood where she had been lying, to see if it could have been the cause of some or all of the cuts and scrapes that had covered the side of Celine's face. He told the jury that the injuries suggested that the first blow had been to the front of the head and she had then received two further blows while she was lying on her front. The Cawley family watched him intently as he told the court that the lack of skull fractures or bleeding inside the skull would suggest that her injuries would not necessarily have been fatal. He said the devastating words matter of factly.

'It is possible her life may have been saved if she had received prompt medical treatment.'

Brendan Grehan stood up, spoiling for a fight. He took exception to Dr Curtis's extrapolation of the course of events, which put his client in a particularly bad light. Since there was no fracture of the skull or bleeding within it, he put it to the pathologist that this would suggest that only moderate force had been behind the blows. Dr Curtis, experienced in giving evidence, didn't miss a beat.

'I think that is a very favourable phrase to use.'

Mr Grehan pushed home his point – establishing that

the force had been moderate was an important distinction to lodge in the minds of the jury.

'But you don't disagree?'

'No.'

His first point won, Mr Grehan closed in on the subject of postural asphyxia. What was it exactly? Dr Curtis was more than happy to explain.

'When someone is unconscious or when we are at rest, our breathing is carried out by the diaphragm. When we are exerting ourselves we also use our chest muscles.' But if someone was unconscious or asleep in a position where the diaphragm was unable to move properly, without the waking movement of the chest muscles they would become deprived of oxygen.

'And that was a factor in this case?'

'It might well have been.'

Mr Grehan pursued his point. How long would this take to happen? A few minutes, possibly a bit longer, came the reply. And was there a greater chance of this happening if the person was obese, he asked. Dr Curtis agreed. Celine Cawley's heart was enlarged and so her body would have had more difficulty coping with a lack of oxygen. Mr Grehan eased home his point – that without these contributory factors death would have been much less likely. Dr Curtis agreed, rather abruptly.

Mr Grehan moved on to the next bone of contention, the marks on Ms Cawley's face. In Dr Curtis's opinion they were clearly caused by her face scraping against a rough surface while her head was struck from behind. Mr Grehan immediately asked him about his visit to Rowan Hill. Had the gardaí shown Dr Curtis the blood spatters on the wall next to the living room window? Dr Curtis shook his head. He had no recollection of any blood spatters. What about the injuries Lillis had when he was arrested? Dr Curtis replied rather sharply that he didn't deal with injuries to the living. Mr Grehan moved swiftly back to deal with Celine's injuries once again. He asked Dr Curtis if he was correct in thinking that the pathologist did not think any of the three head wounds could have been caused by a fall.

'I think that the one in the right frontal temporal region and left occipital parietal region are at sites not typical of a fall.'

The third wound, to the back of the head, could have been the result of a fall, he clarified. Mr Grehan pressed his case. This wasn't a cut and dried diagnosis. There was no way of knowing that the account Lillis had given to Jean Treacy and to his daughter wasn't true. There was a bruise on Celine's back; she could have fallen onto her back, he postulated.

'It was small, only 2cm by 1cm,' Dr Curtis replied. 'If there'd been a fall onto the back I would have expected to see more injury to the back.'

What about if she had fallen onto her head, breaking her fall? Mr Grehan queried.

'I would still expect more bruising.'

Dr Curtis's irritation with the defence counsel was showing.

'I don't think she sustained the three wounds from a single fall, and I don't think that she fell three times, and I think two of those wounds are in positions that are not typical of skull wounds caused by falls.'

Lillis leaned forward and handed a note to his solicitor,

which was duly passed to Mr Grehan. He queried the sequence of events Dr Curtis had put forward. Why did he think that Celine Cawley had been hit on the front of the head first?

'She was found face down.'

'How do you know?'

'I was told that.'

'By whom?'

'By a garda.'

Mr Grehan swooped. Was that the only reason he had come to his decision?

'That and the pattern on the face.'

'Which you take to be the decking?'

'Certainly it is a possibility.'

'But as a pathologist can you really give this view?'

Dr Curtis stood his ground, saying it was a logical interpretation of the facts. Mr Grehan pushed again, suggesting that it was impossible to say for definite. Dr Curtis repeated his view that Celine did not fall three times or sustain her injuries in a single fall. He had been informed that she was lying on her front and her facial injuries supported that. Mr Grehan circled for his final hit. Was Dr Curtis's theory the only possible sequence of events? Dr Curtis looked at him and responded simply.

'Of course not.'

He agreed that if Celine had not been found face down it would be impossible to say the sequence in which the head injuries were sustained. Mr Grehan changed direction, wanting to know whether it was possible that the scrapes to Celine's face had been caused by the pebble-dashed wall. He asked Dr Curtis to have a look at the photograph of the blood spatters on the white wall of the house. Could this have been where the injury occurred? Dr Curtis looked at the photograph before replying that a forensic scientist would be better placed to answer. Mr Grehan wasn't giving up. If Ms Cawley had not been lying on her front, was there any basis for assuming Dr Curtis's sequence of events? Then he delivered the *coup de grace*.

'If the sequence was as you described, if, in fact, she was lying on her front and she received two further heavy blows to the back of the head ... if it happened like that, you would expect far more damage.'

Dr Curtis shook his head. 'If the brick was wielded, we agreed with moderate force, so not necessarily.'

Mr Grehan sat down, having made his point, to a degree. Justice White leaned forward from his bench to look down on Dr Curtis. If a person was struck from the front, what direction would they fall in? It could be either way, Dr Curtis explained, either forwards, or it was possible that a person could fall to their knees and then fall backwards.

'There are no hard and fast rules.'

The next morning Dr Curtis was once again on the stand. Enquiries had been made overnight about who had told him Celine had been found on her back. None of the gardaí had come forward to say that they had given him that information. In fact, a look through the transcript of the trial had unearthed only one mention of what position Celine had been lying in when she died. The 999 call Lillis had made that morning contained a brief reference to the fact that his wife was lying on her side. Justice White leaned forward once again. If the deceased had been found lying on her side, would his sequence still hold?

'I would be less inclined to view the wound which was in the more anterior place as being the first in the sequence.'

This meant that it was less likely that Celine had been hit from the front first.

What about the postural asphyxia? Justice White asked.

Dr Curtis explained that recent studies showed that in obese people the condition was possible whatever position an obese person was lying in. Finally there were no more questions and Dr Curtis could leave the stand.

Ms Ring stayed standing after the pathologist had climbed down and taken a seat at the back of the court. The prosecution case was now at an end, she announced. The press benches seethed with anticipation. We were heading inexorably towards the climax and, finally, a verdict. Mr Grehan got to his feet to announce that the defence intended to produce evidence, an option not always exercised in trials of this nature, and the excitement rose even more. Speculation had been mounting since the jury were sworn in about whether or not Lillis would take the stand himself. There had been a succession of men on trial in the Central Criminal Court in the two years before Celine Cawley died, accused of murdering their wives. After the high profile trials of Joe O'Reilly, Brian Kearney and David Bourke, both the media and the public were well versed on the washing of marital dirty laundry in court. It was natural to compare and contrast the different approaches and outcomes. It was generally agreed that taking the stand was the best course of action for a man accused of killing his wife. But before that question could be answered, the press would need to take down the evidence of one of their own.

Photographer Colin Keegan looked rather uncomfortable as he walked past Lillis to take the stand in his defence. His normal position was outside the courthouse, waiting to snap any of the principal performers in the media circus. He had been one of the press pack that followed Lillis to his earliest court appearances and his name had appeared beside many a photograph of Lillis looking aloof, or the obligatory 'house of death' shots of the scene of the crime. It was one of these photographs that Mr Grehan was interested in. There was a particular shot taken from the paparazzi's favourite vantage point down the laneway at the side of Rowan Hill. It was the only view of the house that wasn't blocked by security gates, or in those days in December 2008, by the garda forensics team. The shot that was shown to the jury was looking across a gap in the hedge onto the decking area where Celine had died. Mr Keegan explained that the picture had been taken using a standard lens, not a telephoto, from the vantage point down the laneway. It showed a clear view of the decking. In cross examination by the prosecution, however, the photographer agreed with Ms Ring that although the front edge of the decking could be seen, what happened further back and close to the ground was not visible from that angle. Mr Keegan quickly left the stand and exited the court to resume his usual role.

But this evidence was little more than the drum roll before the main event, and no sooner had he departed than Mr Grehan stood up and announced the name everyone had been hoping to hear – Eamonn Lillis.

Lillis rose and made his way to the witness box. All eyes in the court were now riveted on him. He raised his hand to take the oath, his face slightly reddened in the glare of all the attention. He bit the insides of his cheeks as he waited for the oath to be read out, then repeated it in a clipped, quiet voice. Mr Grehan got to his feet and smiled at his client before advising him to keep his voice up so that the jury didn't miss a syllable. Lillis nodded, but as he answered the questions on his childhood, his low muttering couldn't be heard beyond the front rows of benches. The jury leaned forward in their seats, frowning with concentration as they tried to keep up with the rapid delivery. Lillis gabbled through his upbringing in Terenure and his educational achievements. Mr Grehan reminded him once more to slow down and speak up as the frustration was beginning to show on the faces of the jury as they missed the details of how he met his wife. Lillis slowed down and leaned closer to the microphone. His eyes darted to the desk in front of him as if longing to fix themselves there. Wearing his customary black suit and white shirt, there was a severity in his stiff pose and clenched jaw. He told the hushed court how he had met Celine Cawley when she organized a football match between Ireland and the rest of the world among the advertising agencies attending the Shark Awards in Kinsale. He spoke of their shared love of German Shepherds and the hurried romance on their return to Dublin. They were both old enough to do without a long engagement, he said; they knew what they wanted.

His voice dropped again as he rushed through the setting up of Toytown Films and his own eventual involvement. He had been freelancing as an artistic director, but there were cash flow problems. Celine had suggested he join the fold and start learning the ropes. She had persuaded him with flattery, telling him he could be an asset to the agency. The press benches leaned forward so as not to miss a word as he finally praised the woman who had been his wife for seventeen years, saying that Celine was an extremely good producer and highly regarded in the industry. He lowered his head and muttered through the list of houses they had lived in as a married couple.

But Mr Grehan didn't dwell on history. He quickly brought questioning round to the crux of the matter by way of the daily texts between Lillis and his lover, at around 9.30 each morning.

'That's right,' Lillis agreed stiffly, pausing to clarify, 'not every morning.'

But they were due to meet on the morning of 15 December 2008, Mr Grehan pressed. There had been an exchange of texts the night before, arranging a meeting?

'That's correct, yeah. We had arranged to meet up in town.'

Lillis spoke stiffly, hardly moving his lips. The press benches leaned forward to catch the hurried words as he clarified details of the meeting, muttering something about going into town to get new lights for the Christmas tree. Yet again, his barrister reminded him to slow down and speak up. There was an arrangement to meet that morning, he prompted.

'That's right, yeah.'

Mr Grehan led Lillis through his morning routine. The waking up around 6.45 and making tea for his wife and daughter after he had done his sit ups for the day. The courtroom was hushed. This was the first account of the row on that morning that was actually from the horse's mouth. Lillis went on describing his morning, painting a picture of marital harmony. He had brought Celine her tea, he told the court, and stayed there for a 'kiss and a cuddle' before going upstairs for his shower. After breakfast he had dropped his daughter to school, in the Mercedes ML, the car that everyone was now familiar with as the vehicle favoured by his mistress for the added leg room and darkened windows. The Cawley family listened patiently as Lillis revisited his comings and goings and as the narrative moved slowly towards the inevitable climax. Lillis told about walking the dogs and eventually reached his return home. His voice was even more clipped as he described his arrival and discovery of a bag of rubbish waiting for him to dispose of it. His account was detailed, taking care of every point that had been raised during the trial.

Celine had been washing out the fridge, he told the jury, so she was wearing rubber gloves. She was still wearing the gloves when she came out after him once the row started. Once again, he highlighted his own innocence: the dutiful husband, grabbing an old pair of gloves with the intention of going out to 'de-poo' the garden when Celine started the row. She had asked him if he had put out meal worms for the robin. Suddenly the significance of the perplexing questions about meal worms to both Jean Treacy and Lillis's daughter became clear. Both of them had said the argument was about putting out the rubbish, but Lillis himself was raising the matter of the robin. Sitting rigidly in the witness box, he clenched his jaw as he described that last row. He had told his wife he hadn't put out the bird food, he informed the court. She had asked him why not, as he had been asked to do this three days ago. Already it was sounding like any normal marital spat. Lillis told the court he had gone outside, putting on the gloves as he went, but Celine followed him angrily. She had shouted after him:

'That's just bloody typical of you. You keep forgetting things.'

He sounded uncomfortable repeating the angry words.

Mr Grehan stepped in.

'So there was an argument, basically?'

'It was back and forth, yes.'

Lillis said he started 'hurling some abuse at her' which made Celine 'quite angry'. But he hadn't seen her fall.

'I saw Celine getting up off the ground and she picked up a brick. She was rubbing the back of her head with her hand.'

His tone of voice didn't alter as he described asking her if she was ok. But the tension in his voice was obvious as he played back her irritated response.

'What do you care? What do you care?'

Lillis said that the row flared again and Celine shoved the brick at him.

'When I came close to her she was angry with me.'

'Did she make contact?' Mr Grehan asked.

'No I actually grabbed it out of her hand.'

He said that at this point he attempted to walk away from the row, but his wife shouted after him. Once again, the angry words sounded stilted as he spoke them awkwardly back to the court.

'That's just typical of you. You always walk away when we have a row.'

The row continued, he said, and became 'extremely vocal and extremely nasty'. Lillis said he turned and went back towards his wife, thrusting the brick out in her direction, with the suggestion, 'Why don't you shove this where the sun doesn't shine.'

His wife then got really angry. He was also fairly incandescent, he said, and was jabbing her shoulder with his finger. The two of them were shouting and screaming insults at each other. Then things got really physical when his wife grabbed the brick from him and swung it.

'I don't think she actually meant to hit me but she caught me on the side of my face. I got extremely angry then and I pushed her back towards the two sliding doors.'

He said he was trying to grab the brick out of her hand when 'my left glove shot off my hand.'

The Cawley family sat in silence, listening as Lillis explained how he himself was injured.

'My hand caught the brick again. I cut my finger on it and my fingernail got torn off ... I didn't realise what was wrong at the time, just felt that my finger had been hurt but I was extremely angry. I pushed her again quite hard, pushed her up against the corner of the window.'

At this point he said Celine let out an 'almighty scream', presumably the same scream that had woken neighbour Pauline Fraser after her late night. Lillis said he didn't know whether the scream had been a scream of pain or anger, and that Celine had twisted around in his grip.

'She caught me with the brick again. She had her arm raised to try and fend me off.'

He grabbed Celine's right arm, which was holding the brick, and pushed it back across her right shoulder.

'She started twisting round sideways to get away from me.'

By this stage, Lillis said, they were over towards the edge of the decking by the patio when he slipped on the icy ground. He fell to his knees and Celine fell backwards, with him still holding on to her.

'Her knees crumpled and she sort of fell down.'

Lillis was still speaking quietly and quickly, hardly moving his jaw.

'She was lying on the ground, flat on her back. I was on my knees, sort of across her.'

He said that the fall had knocked the wind out of both of them and the row was suddenly over. He tried to get up, but as he did, Celine bit down hard on his little finger, shaking her head from side to side like a dog worrying a bone. He told the attentive courtroom that he then put the heel of his hand on her forehead to push her head down onto the decking and stop her from moving. He said the brick was lying on the ground somewhere near her head where it had fallen when she fell. She kept moving her head from side to side and biting down on his finger. With meticulous attention to detail, Lillis explained that his other glove had become trapped under Celine's body and now fell off his hand. He was in pain, he said, and extremely angry. He smacked her forehead back but she kept biting down. He commented that the brick was still quite close by. He said that, suddenly, Celine let go of his finger and 'things stopped'.

'I picked up the brick because it was very close to her head, and threw it.'

Mr Grehan went back over the last stage. They had fallen half on and half off the decking. Celine had kept turning her head and he had used the heel of his hand to stop her moving? Lillis agreed.

'I held her head down to the ground so she couldn't move her head. Then she opened her mouth.'

'Why?' Mr Grehan wanted to know.

'I don't know, she just stopped.' He paused, then noted that there was some blood on the ground by her head.

'Was that the first time you noticed blood?'

'Yes, it was actually.'

Lillis said he got to his knees, but Celine seemed 'kind of quiet or dazed or something'.

'She went to sit up and I could see her head was cut.'

So far, according to his account, he was blameless in the matter of his wife's injuries. Lillis went on that he persuaded her to rest her head on his lap.

Mr Grehan asked him why he had done that.

'Because she seemed dazed. I was just looking after her the way I always had. I didn't know what I was doing.'

He said Celine had rested her head on his lap for just a

few seconds before sitting up again. Mr Grehan asked if the row had just disappeared. Lillis said it had, after they had fallen.

'I think it was the shock of what had happened. We had had rows over the years but we had never had a fight.'

Mr Grehan asked him to account for his wife's injuries – how had she sustained three separate head wounds and significant grazes to her face? Lillis chewed his lip as he formulated his answer.

'I assume the first time she fell she struck her head on the brick because she was holding it. The second time, when I pushed her up against the window, she must have hit her head, because she let out a scream.'

He turned his attention to the scrapes on her face. These would have happened, he explained, when the brick grazed her face as he raised her arm above her head when they struggled. Finally 'The third time she banged her head was more than likely when we fell on the decking. There was certainly blood.'

The barrister asked him about the marks on his own face – the three scratches that had run down the length of his face. Lillis answered fluidly.

'That happened the two times she hit my face with the brick.'

But what about the nail marks? Mr Grehan queried.

'She scratched my face after we fell down the last time.'

Lillis said that once the row stopped he sat on the decking thinking about what had just happened. He assumed his wife was also contemplating what had occurred. She didn't speak at first, but after a moment she sat up and pulled off the remaining rubber glove. He said he asked Celine what on earth they were going to tell their daughter, but she didn't turn towards him to answer. He said she just said, 'yeah, yeah' and told him to go away. The house had been burgled about a year and a half before, he said, so the idea of a burglary came to mind naturally. He told the court he said to his wife:

'What a disaster. What do you think, and she went "yeah, yeah" and waved her hand at me.'

Lillis said he got up and went back into the kitchen, returning a couple of seconds later with some damp kitchen roll that had been left on the draining board by

Celine when she was cleaning the fridge, and a tea towel. He also wrapped his bleeding finger in a piece of tissue. Celine was still sitting on the decking so he asked her again if she was all right. He said she replied:

'Yeah, yeah, just fuck off and leave me alone. Go away, go away.'

He felt he needed to get away, he said, to give the air a chance to clear. He could see that her head was bleeding but there didn't seem to be a lot of blood. 'I didn't think she was incredibly injured.'

He told the jury he picked up the bloody kitchen towels that Celine had used to mop the blood from her head and the gloves that were lying around the decking and put them in a plastic bin bag that was in the kitchen. Then he went into the living room and the cupboard where the camera stuff was kept, to fake the robbery. He selected a couple of cameras, a lens and a video camera and took them with him when he went upstairs to clean himself up. After having a wash in the bathroom, he went into his bedroom. He took off his watch and put it on the bedside table, then noticed that there was blood on his jeans. He changed into a t-shirt and a pair of combat jeans, throwing his bloody clothes on the floor. Then, he said, he went back into the bathroom.

'I sat on the edge of the bath, just trying to gather myself. I was incredibly upset and in quite a bit of pain as well.'

He went back into the bedroom and decided that the clothes were too bloody to wash, so he put them all in a bin bag on the landing. There was a small suitcase there as well so he shoved the bin bag and the camera equipment into the case and into the open attic.

Why had he gone to all this trouble? Mr Grehan asked.

'I knew the moment I came downstairs Celine would ask me, if we were going to make it look like a robbery, what are you going to do about it.'

He told the jury he went downstairs because he knew he and Celine would have to have a serious talk about what had happened.

'I wanted to see where she was, see what she was up to, so I went back into the kitchen. I looked out the door and I saw Celine was lying on the ground.' He took a quick breath before continuing. 'I went out to her and I called her name.' There was a catch in his voice as he carried on. 'She was mostly on her back, her arms and her legs and her head were facing sideways. I called her name ...' He sucked in a convulsive breath. 'I called her name and she didn't answer me.' Another breath. 'So I ...' It seemed too painful to carry on. 'I knelt down beside her and I shook her chin. She didn't wake up and I called her name again.' He took another breath and rubbed his eyes with a finger. His eyes were red but dry of tears.

'Could you see if she was breathing?' Mr Grehan asked gently.

Lillis sniffed deeply before continuing. 'I kept calling her name and checked her pulse in her neck and her wrist but I couldn't feel her pulse.' Despite the rapid breaths, Lillis's tone was measured, the same rapid monotone rush in which he had delivered all his evidence. 'I ran back inside and got on the phone and I called the ambulance.'

Had he told the emergency operator that there had been an intruder?

'Yes I did, because that's what I said to Celine we were going to say.' He rushed on. 'I couldn't work out if she was conscious. I didn't think it was too serious, even then I thought surely she was going to be OK. There was no reason I could think that she would go from being reasonably OK to seriously injured.'

Lillis went on to describe his attempts to save Celine, helped by the arrival of the emergency services. Mr Grehan led him carefully back over various details and clarifications to his story before approaching the matter of the lies. Why had he lied to gardaí and not told them what had happened? Lillis looked at him with a sincere expression and rattled off his answer.

'It's going to sound awful, but again I assumed Celine was going to be fine.' He said he couldn't believe it when he had been told she was dead. 'I went into complete shock. I didn't know what to do.'

'You made a very lengthy statement describing a masked intruder.'

'I was trying to deny what happened. I didn't want people to know we had a fight. People already thought there had been a burglar. I just got paralysed. I'm sorry.'

Brendan Grehan reminded him that he had told the story not just once but had rung gardaí the following day to add details.

'Having said it, I just didn't see any way out. I felt I had no way out of it. All Celine's family and all of Celine's friends – I just felt completely trapped and I couldn't see any way out. I had boxed myself into a corner.'

Mr Grehan asked again why he hadn't admitted his mistake.

'I had never been in a situation like this in my life, never any kind of violence. Especially a situation like this – you know, my wife was dead. I couldn't believe it. I didn't want to accept it even, and having said it, I couldn't find any way to explain what had happened.'

Why had it taken until January for him to tell his daughter what had really happened? Mr Grehan asked.

'I had been thinking about it all through December and January. I couldn't not tell her.'

He was almost finished telling his story now. In a few minutes he would face the prosecution in his cross examination, but for now he was still in the gentle hands of his own counsel. In closing, Mr Grehan brought his client round to the mysterious notes found on his bedside table.

'They were some notes I had made several weeks before. It was a treatment for a script I was doing.' He looked at his barrister earnestly. 'It was based on things in my life, but it wasn't to do with subsequent events.'

With that, his story was at an end.

Mr Grehan sat down and the far less well-disposed Ms Ring took his place. She stood for a while, looking at Lillis on the stand. He looked back at her levelly.

'Do you remember yesterday?' she asked him coolly.

'Yes.'

'"I was brought up never to lie." Do you remember your daughter saying that?'

Lillis seemed a little taken aback at her question, but his response when she asked if he had taken an active part in his daughter's upbringing was swift, with a first flash of what may have been anger.

'I was present throughout her childhood.'

Why, then, had he lied throughout his dealings with gardaí and the emergency services? Slowly and deliberately she started to list his lies for the jury. The first was at 10.04 when he had told Kevin Moran, who answered the 999 call, that he and his wife had been attacked by an intruder.

'Was that the first lie?'

Lillis agreed, rather curtly.

'Gardaí arrived at 10.10. Shortly afterwards, at 10.25, you gave Inspector Angela Willis a description of an intruder in dark clothes and gloves. That was a lie.'

Next was the lie to Detective Sergeant Gary Kelly, describing the 'intruder' as a man, 5'11" tall, and wearing jeans and a balaclava.

'That is another lie.'

On the stand Lillis looked like a chastised schoolboy.

'Yes.'

Ms Ring continued cataloguing the lies. Lillis had gone with gardaí to Howth garda station and handed over his t-shirt and the combats that he said he had been wearing all day.

'That's the fourth lie.'

'Yes.'

'You committed to writing a statement on the 15th December which is some five typewritten pages. That is the fifth lie.'

'Yes.'

'In that you make reference to a man, you gave a man to gardaí. That man had nothing to do with the death of your wife. Was that the sixth lie?'

'I did not try to implicate him in Celine's death. I did not try to implicate him.'

'We heard about raw grief from yourself and [your daughter].'

Something in Lillis seemed to crack, and for the first time the emotion rushed out.

'I felt completely and utterly trapped. I just did not want anyone to know we had fought. I am truly, truly sorry. I couldn't see a way out of it. Literally every minute of every day I just couldn't see a way out of it.'

His passion fell on deaf ears as Ms Ring relentlessly pursued her line of questioning.

'Did you allow the lie to continue with your daughter?'

Lillis was passionate in his defence of his stance with his daughter.

'I did. We had already concocted that story to protect her.'

'Was that the sixth lie?'

'I presume so.'

Ms Ring was not yet near the end of her list.

'There were a number of people who met up on the 15th December 2008 and you spoke to them. You continued the story about the burglary. That is the seventh lie.'

'Siobhan O'Farrell [the sister of Chris Cawley's wife, Sorcha] talked about seeing you and you explaining how you lost your nail as you grabbed the rucksack of the intruder. That was the eighth lie, on the 15th December. On the 16th December you phone the gardaí because you had now remembered something: that you had blacked out.'

Lillis stared straight ahead.

'Yes. I was in a complete and total panic at the time.'

Ms Ring did not pause.

'That is now the ninth lie.'

'I was making the situation far worse for myself and everybody else. I just did not know what to do.'

Ms Ring did not ease up. She told Lillis he had lied about holding his wife's hand to his face.

'I didn't want to tell them that Celine scratched my face.'

Unmoved, she reminded him that he had a conversation with Chris Cawley about an article in the *Evening Herald* and had failed to tell him there had been no intruder, and so had continued the lie. Even after his arrest on 20 December, when it should have been apparent to him that the gardaí did not believe the intruder story, he had continued to lie.

Lillis was now rather red in the face.

'I didn't know what to do. I had never been in a situation like this. I was taking stuff during that time. I was taking Valium, sleeping pills. I was irrational.'

Ms Ring paused and looked at him.

'You are a fifty-two-year-old adult. Your child, a seventeen-year-old, knows you do not lie.'

She brushed away Lillis's protestations and looked at him coldly.

'You were well used to lying and deception, weren't you? You had been lying for eight weeks.'

Lillis wet his lips nervously, his mouth pursing before he answered.

'I wasn't lying to her.'

Ms Ring did not let up.

'Did you tell her when you went into town to go shopping you were also meeting Jean Treacy?'

Lillis's shot back a piece of classic adulterous doublethink.

'I wasn't telling her lies. I wasn't lying to her.'

What about the telephones, Ms Ring pressed, the one had bought for himself and for Jean Treacy to conduct their affair?

'Was that deception?'

Lillis had no choice but to agree, but he immediately tried to qualify his answer.

'I was deceiving her by not telling her. I didn't lie directly about it.'

Ms Ring didn't comment. She had moved on, wanting to know about his conversation with his daughter. Had he told her the truth?

'I didn't give her every single detail, but I told her what happened.'

But his daughter had been under the impression that the row had been over rubbish, Ms Ring pressed. Lillis stubbornly replied:

'She got that confused. I did mention it to her.'

The whole story of the intruder was faked, Ms Ring repeated once more. She queried whether he was suggesting that, if his wife's wounds were not caused by an intruder, they were self inflicted?

'Are you saying none of that was caused by you?'

'It was caused by the struggle between us when we had a row.'

Ms Ring asked him how long he had been away from his wife while she was seriously injured out on the patio. Less than fifteen minutes, came the answer. Why had he thrown out his clothes? They were too bloody. Why had he wiped his wife's blood off his watch? He hadn't, he replied, the blood must have washed off it when he washed his hands. Why had he left his wife lying there, bleeding to death, dying? He hadn't, he replied, she had been sitting up when he left her. He had wanted to give both of them time to calm down. Why had he started covering up for his daughter when she wasn't due home from school for hours? Because Celine would have asked why he hadn't done anything, came the reply. The tension in his voice was audible each time he mentioned Celine's possible reaction.

Ms Ring moved her questioning back to the row itself. She asked where the three dogs had been after their walk. He explained that Molly had gone to lie outside as normal. Sam, the cocker spaniel, had probably gone into their daughter's playroom where he would lie on the beanbag and Harry, the Rhodesian ridgeback, would have been around somewhere. She asked why the dogs hadn't come running when they heard the row. He told her that that simply wouldn't have happened. Gradually Ms Ring was bringing Lillis back to the row itself. She smoothly asked what had caused the row to flare that

December morning.

'She could be very sarcastic. It wasn't the meal worms, it was that I hadn't bothered doing it. She said it was typical of me. It wasn't the food for the robin, it was the fact she had asked me to do something and I hadn't done it.'

Ms Ring asked him what had happened next.

'She came out after me to continue the argument. We had moved on. I told her to "F" off. That's typical of you. And she kind of went out after me.'

'Did she ever know about Jean Treacy?' Ms Ring asked calmly.

'No.'

'Was this a typical argument?'

'We have had arguments of a similar nature over the years, but nothing like this.'

The row had quickly got worse, Lillis told her.

'She started asking me why I hadn't been out generating work for the company.' He said he told her, 'There is no work. We're in the middle of a recession.' The company had been quiet for a couple of months, he explained.

'She said I didn't care for [our daughter] and didn't care

for her.'

'Did that make you angry?'

'It made me very angry, yes.'

Mary Ellen Ring pressed him further.

'You were carrying a secret.'

'That had nothing to do with the argument that day.'

'You were seeing a woman on a regular basis. The phone traffic alone – there had been text contact the night before about arranging a meeting. You are having an argument with your wife. She's making you very angry, but the secret you were carrying had nothing to do with the row you were having?'

Lillis insisted the row had nothing to do with his affair. He had been angry, he said. He had said horrendous things to his wife.

'I told Celine she was only interested in her own image as superwoman. She didn't appreciate stuff she had. All I've been doing here. You don't seem to be appreciating the work I do around the house.'

'Were you resentful?' Ms Ring probed.

'Angry rather than resentful,' came the answer. 'It was

unfair, but then I said a lot of unfair things to her too.'

Ms Ring took him through the struggle again, move by move. Which hand had Celine held the brick in? Which hand had he used? She went through each step of the fight as if she was choreographing a dance. Lillis answered her questions without hesitation. He pointed out where they had been standing according to the crime scene photographs, explained the movements of the brick between them, which hand it had been held in by each of them. Where were they standing when he had told his wife to shove the brick where the sun didn't shine? the barrister asked. Just past the corner of the kitchen. You were facing her? Yes, the brick had been in her right hand. How angry had he been? He had been extremely angry. His finger had been hurt and she had hit him in the face. He had pushed her against the window, hard. It wouldn't have been the window, more the edge of the window. Had his wife being trying to fend him off? Ms Ring asked him suddenly. Lillis didn't miss a beat.

'I was trying to pull the brick from her hand. She was

trying to stop me. I was trying to grab her arm and stop her swinging the brick. She was trying to avoid me grabbing her arm.'

How had they fallen down? He had been on the paved patio area, Lillis explained, but he had stepped back onto the decking and slipped. He had been holding Celine at the time and had pulled her down with him. In an echo of Dr Curtis's evidence, he described her knees crumpling as she fell backwards. The brick had fallen to the ground beside her, very close to her, he explained. Ms Ring asked him about the finger biting. Why hadn't he mentioned it to gardaí?

'I didn't want to tell the guards we had had a fight.'

'Did you tell the doctor about your finger being bitten?'

'No.'

'Did you tell your daughter about the finger biting?'

'I can't remember. I think I did, actually.'

Ms Ring asked him how he had stopped his wife biting his finger. Had he really used the gentle pressure of the heel of his hand? Lillis repeated how he had held Celine's head to stop her moving while she moved her head from side to side, like a dog worrying a bone. Had he noticed that her head was bleeding?

'I didn't really notice that much until she let go of my finger and sat back up.'

Ms Ring reminded him that head wounds bled profusely. There would have been quite a lot of blood.

'There wasn't as much blood at the time.'

The barrister once again referred to the photographs, pointing out the pool of dried blood that spread across the wooden deck. Then she closed in for the attack. The brick had been saturated with blood and there had been a long dark hair sticking to it. Lillis spoke quickly.

'It would have picked up blood where it was lying. When I threw it to one side.'

Ms Ring pounced. The brick had picked up the blood but he had not noticed any blood on his wife's head? Lillis took a drink of water, his little finger crooked as he held the glass, his mouth pursed. He paused for several seconds. Ms Ring gave him a prompt.

'Celine seemed quiet or distant. She sat up. You saw her head.'

'She was resting her head on my lap,' he agreed.

'Explain to the jury about the blood on your jeans.'

'I'm not too sure where that came from.'

She pressed him further. Hadn't he noticed the blood when he got up to go upstairs?

'I was in quite a state.'

Why hadn't he come downstairs when he had seen how much blood was on his jeans?

'At the time I was thinking, I was just in my head trying to work out what the heck we had done. I wasn't thinking like that at the time.'

But he had known that his wife's head was cut and bleeding, Ms Ring insisted. Hadn't he at least checked she was ok?

'I asked her was she ok. I just saw blood in her hair.'

'You didn't ask her could you look at it. She couldn't see the back of her head.'

'No.'

'You could see the back of her head was covered in blood.'

'I presumed she knew.'

'Did you now go back down to her when you saw the blood when you changed upstairs?'

Lillis replied that he had assumed she only had one cut. Once again Ms Ring itemised his actions to him. There had been three lacerations, she told him. The first when Celine fell and hit her head with the brick; he had seen her getting up and rubbing the back of her head. The second laceration was when he had pushed her against the window frame and she had cried out. The third laceration had happened when she fell again and when he had pushed her head down onto the deck.

'No, I didn't use that much force on her then.'

Ms Ring reminded him that he had told gardaí that Celine had scratched his face 'as a cat would do'.

'Was that part of her trying to fend you off?'

'No, it was after we fell.'

'Did she attack you because you were attacking her?'

'It was part of the fight.'

Ms Ring nodded. The fight in which Lillis had received injuries that had needed hospital treatment? Yes, he nodded, his fingernail had been torn off. The fight that had left the emergency services fighting to save his wife's life?

'That was never said at the time.'

The courtroom clock showed a couple of minutes after 4 o'clock. Ms Ring went for the big finish.

'You didn't need any medical assistance. You didn't have any lacerations on your body. Between 9.30 on the 15th December 2008 until sometime shortly after 10.04 the only person who's here to tell us about what exactly happened is yourself.'

Lillis looked at her.

'That's true.'

The court took time to empty as the crowds spilled out into the corridor. The Cawley family looked slightly shellshocked; Celine's father had obviously found the account of his daughter's violent death very difficult to take. His children stayed protectively close to him as the court emptied, before moving out. Lillis stayed behind to talk to his counsel. He would have an uncomfortable weekend waiting for the second round of questioning.

CHAPTER 8

From the Horse's Mouth

On Monday morning the crowd was bigger than ever as a result of the Sunday papers' coverage of Lillis's first day of evidence. An hour before the court was due to open, the audience had arrived, massing around the double doors and jostling to get to the front of the queue. The media crowd had also grown as the trial came closer to its conclusion. The journalists stood at an aloof distance from the throngs of public, but when the doors opened to allow them in ahead, there was still a school-kid rush to the best seats. Lillis came in a short time later, taking his seat in his enclosure and biting his lip nervously as the court filled up. Once again the crowds were six or seven deep at the back of the courtroom. The overflow room, which was really the room where the jury panel gathered before being called to selection, was in use as always on a Monday, so the crowd spilled right out into the corridor outside the court. Someone had come with a guide dog, a patient black Labrador that lay at his master's feet and narrowly avoided being trodden on in the crush. Mary Ellen Ring stopped to scratch him behind the ears as she made her way to the front of the court, a brief chink in the stern persona she assumed when prosecuting.

This morning she had good reason to look stern. Apart from the second leg of her cross examination of Lillis, a serious legal issue had arisen over the weekend. A ripple of concern passed around the press benches as pages from a newspaper were visible on the desk in front of each counsel, folded to obscure the masthead from general view. The solicitor for the *Independent* group came forward and journalists for the papers within that group could be seen mentally checking what they'd written in the past week. There was a swell of relief when it became clear who had slipped up. Along the bench the pens started scratching away to catch a colleague's chastisement. The *Evening Herald* was in the firing line, having inadvertently named Lillis's daughter in the Friday edition of the paper. The solicitor offered the paper's sincere apologies and said that the paper was happy to hold up its hands and take the blame. He offered his assurances that it was an honest mistake. It was unfortunate that the reference had slipped through but there was 'nothing sinister' about the appearance of the girl's name. The other journalists shot sympathetic glances towards their unfortunate colleague. But time was ticking by and Justice White stayed the axe until another date. The jury took their seats.

Mary Ellen Ring got back to her feet and announced her attention to pick up where she had left off. She quizzed Lillis on his wife's position when he found her collapsed. Was he one hundred per cent sure she was on her side? He was. Then how had she come to have abrasions to the front of her face? It must have been the brick grazing her face when he pulled her arm back, he replied. That was the only time he could think of that it could have happened. Ms Ring went back over each of the scratches and wounds that Celine had when she died, with an increasing air of bemusement. Why was it that two of the head wounds had been horizontal when Lillis was saying that at least one had been caused by the perpendicular window surround? Lillis frowned seriously in the witness box. He had no idea why that would be the case. The barrister moved on to the blood-stained clothes. There had been a lot of blood there. Did he really expect the jury to believe that he hadn't noticed more blood? Lillis stuck to his story. What about the blood on his jumper, Ms Ring asked. How had that got there? Lillis explained that when Celine had rested her head on his lap it had not simply been on his lap, as he had said on Friday. He had also held her head against his chest. That must have been where the blood came from. Ms Ring was still sounding bemused as she questioned him relentlessly. The jury were left in no doubt that she found Lillis's story incredible. She asked about the blood spatters. They were on the wall beside the kitchen door, almost five and half feet off the ground. Celine had been 5'10", which would have meant her head was bent when the blood was spilt.

'She was actually 5'8" ,' Lillis came back defiantly. 'I was married to her and she was 5'8". '

Ms Ring ignored his protest. She went back to the burglary story. Had Lillis really made this up for his daughter's benefit? Surely he was trying to cover up for when the gardaí were called in? Lillis insisted he had not known his wife was seriously injured. There had never been any suggestion that the gardaí would be called. Ms Ring was still finding it hard to believe that he would not have gone to check on his injured wife. The irritation was showing as Lillis responded sharply to the repetitive questions. He hadn't known she was seriously injured, he insisted, and besides:

'Considering how rude and what she said to me when I left her, I didn't feel like shouting down to her.'

Ms Ring was not impressed. If the whole thing had been an accident, why hadn't Lillis told the gardaí? He had felt trapped, he repeated. But the gardaí had given him repeated opportunities to admit what had happened in the days and weeks that had followed, she pointed out. Had his feeling 'trapped' had any other cause?

'You were trapped because you had a new opportunity of a life with Miss Treacy,' she suggested.

Lillis's reply came back sharply.

'There was never a possibility. That was never going to happen.'

Ms Ring went back to the note found on the desk. There were far too many similarities to the reality of the situation for that to be fiction, she stated. Lillis sprang to his own defence. It *was* fiction. He had been writing a script. He had complete backup notes and journals to prove he had been writing one.

'That's part of the character development.'

The note had said 'you are running out of time'. It had referred to a house in France. He and Celine had a house in France.

'Again it doesn't refer to our situation at all.'

He started a complicated explanation of ideas and scripts. It had all started when they had been filming for the Irish Permanent Building Society, he said. They were filming a bank robbery and some passersby had thought they were reconstructing a crime. He had thought it would be an amusing idea to write a script about a film crew who actually did rob a bank under the pretence of making a film of robbing a bank. The note had come about when he had woken up in the middle of the night with an idea based on his own experiences. He told the jury he had thought:

'That makes a very simple idea for a script.'

He had been going to take the pages of notepaper into the office to work on them further. It had never been about him.

'It was simply sparked off by the situation I was involved in.'

The story had been about two different characters running out of time, he explained. He had just dashed off the notes, but they were mainly fiction.

'I had no time for it. I had no reason to be trapped.'

Ms Ring did not relent.

'I have to put it to you that the three injuries on Celine Cawley's head occurred by the use of a brick held by you and you lied to the ambulance, gardaí, your family and your friends. You continued that lie. The reason you lied was all because you had taken the brick and hit her, not once, not twice, but three times. Three lacerations consistent with a brick, not a window, and you lied to cover up the incident that had happened on the patio.'

'That's not true.'

Ms Ring sat down and Mr Grehan stood up. That was the end of the defence, he explained. There was an excited murmur through the court as the watchers realised that the trial was in its final stages. The speeches would start the next morning and a verdict would not be long in coming. The jury were allowed home before the task ahead of them the following day, but the rest of the court stayed sitting. Before the closing arguments began, there were some important legal issues to hammer out. Mr Grehan had a major problem with the prosecution's case. He told Justice White that there had been no evidence that a murder had been committed, so that option should not be given to the jury. He said that Ms Ring's final suggestion to Lillis had been that he had hit his wife with a brick three times. This was according to the pathologist's evidence, which had been seriously undermined. But when Dr Curtis's account was taken out of the equation there was nothing else to suggest that the brick had been used. The jury would have to be convinced beyond a reasonable doubt that a murder had been committed outside the sequence of events given by Dr Curtis. They couldn't take a leap of faith.

Lillis sat staring into the distance, rubbing his lip with a finger as he listened intently.

Justice White was having none of it. The jury were entitled to infer from the evidence, he told Mr Grehan, even if they couldn't suppose. He was not going to remove the option of murder from the possible verdicts they had.

Mr Grehan got to his feet again. In that case they should have six options open to them based on how much of Lillis's story they had believed. The first option was an acquittal. If they believed his entire testimony, this would have been the only option, since Celine's death would have been nothing more than a tragic accident. If they did not believe him fully, they could choose manslaughter, but here there were four options open to them. Mr Grehan explained that if they had believed Lillis's account of the fight but thought that he had hit his wife with the brick as he was being attacked, then it would be self defence with excessive force. If the jury believed that Lillis had struck his wife because of the things said in the fight, then it would be provocation. The third option was that they believed Lillis had known his wife was seriously injured and had left her to die; this would have been criminal negligence. The fourth option would be that the jury were satisfied Lillis had killed his wife but had not been convinced by the prosecution that he intended to do so. This would mean manslaughter because murder had not been proven.

The judge leaned forward. He would give the jury all the options that Mr Grehan had suggested, but he intended to tell the jury that they must inform him which of the options they had picked. A ruling in the recent case of Taxquent vs. Belgium in the European Court of Human Rights allowed for a judge to direct the jury to explain their decision, and he intended to implement the ruling.

Neither side looked happy as the judge rose and the

court emptied. There would be more arguments the following day.

The next morning, both prosecution and defence were
quick to voice their protests about Justice White's plan
for the jury. As Ms Ring explained to him, the Director of
Public Prosecutions himself was against the ruling
because it encroached on a jury's freedom to deliberate
and pass verdict in private, a premise at the very heart of
the jury system. Ireland had made submissions to the
European Court of Human Rights on the subject and, as
of yet, there had been no ruling to decide the matter. The
judgement on the Taxquent vs. Belgium case had only
been issued in June 2009. Mr Grehan went even further.
He told the judge that the use of a brand new piece of
legislation would be extraordinary in these circumstances, perverse even.

Justice White held firm. He insisted that if the jury were
to be given a variety of ways to arrive at a manslaughter
verdict they should be required to explain which argument had convinced them to make their decision. It
would help the judge decide upon a sentence.

Mr Grehan disagreed. The issue hadn't even been tried in the Court of Criminal Appeal in Ireland.

'I ask that this court does not depart from the normal procedure.'

For once, both prosecution and defence were united. Justice White looked down at them and glanced towards the door that led to the jury room. He would reserve his decision, he said. He clearly wouldn't be starting his part in the closing of the trial until after lunch at the earliest. The barristers sat down and the jury filed in and took their seats. The sketch artists gripped their charcoals and glanced towards Lillis, sitting with his head lowered over his notes. The Cawley family, sitting at the back of the courtroom, exchanged apprehensive glances. Then Mary Ellen Ring got to her feet.

She told the jury that the time had almost come for them to take centre stage. They had been selected to try the facts of the case, and they, and only they, would decide whether Lillis was guilty or not guilty. The jury listened intently as she explained the principle of trial by jury, how each man and women brought to their deliberations a whole life of experience that would aid their judgement. She told them they would have to decide whether Lillis had in fact murdered his wife. Murder in the Irish legal system, she explained, was defined as a negative. She explained that an unlawful killing was not murder unless the person intended to kill or cause serious injury. Regarding intent, she explained that a person was presumed to have intended the 'natural and probable consequences' of his actions. Intent could be fleeting, she told the six men and women who were hanging on her every word, some of them studiously taking note of everything she said. 'We often say "I didn't mean to say that",' she told them, but 'the intention when you opened your mouth and the words came out was to say them.'

The fact that a person was remorseful did not undo their intent. In the prosecution's opinion, she told them, this was a straightforward case. Lillis had taken an opportunity to murder his wife when it was presented and had then done everything in his power to cover up his actions.

'Looking at the stage where we say he was holding the brick in his hands – that's intention. Not where he dials 999, but with the brick in his hands applying moderate force.'

Lillis watched her intently as her speech continued, his lips pursed. His gaze was as focused as the jury's although he was not, at this stage, taking the same copious notes.

Ms Ring told the jury that even though Dr Curtis had agreed that his theory about the sequence of Celine's injuries might have been mistaken, he was still satisfied that her injuries had been caused by a blunt instrument and that she had not sustained them in a single fall or in three separate falls. The position she had been found in did not alter his findings. She reminded them that Lillis himself had said he was extremely angry but had not suggested that he was out of control. They must be satisfied to a very high degree to convict of anything, she told them. Their decision must be beyond reasonable doubt. This was required by law, not as a favour to the accused.

'This isn't a long planned-out murder mystery, but an

opportunity presented itself on the morning of the 15th of December and Mr Lillis took that opportunity and he took up the brick and hit Celine Cawley on three occasions with moderate force ... and having done that he went upstairs calmly, and in a collected fashion washed his hands, changed his clothes and washed his watch. He then went to get camera equipment.'

It was only after doing all of this, she told the attentive jury, that he went back to his wife and found her dying. 'At that stage perhaps the panic sets in.' He had called the gardaí and created an intruder holding a brick in his hand.

'This is murder, not some unfortunate accident. This is not a man who lost control of himself, rather a man who was presented with an opportunity and acted on it.'

The true verdict in this case, she told them, was that Eamonn Lillis, on December 15th 2008, had murdered Celine Cawley.

Ms Ring took her seat and there was a brief, silent pause before Mr Grehan stood to speak for the defence. He turned his back on his client in order to face the jury and put his foot up on the bench beside him. He cut straight to the chase.

'I am asking you to acquit him.'

But, he said, he *would* say that, being Lillis's counsel. Several of the jurors looked at him with very unconvinced expressions. Others smiled at the sudden release in tension. Mr Grehan told them he was not going to ask them to acquit based on anything he was going to say. But, he said, if the jury were to look closely at the case put by the prosecution they would find it did not stand up to any scrutiny. This was not a case where someone's head was battered in with a brick. Celine Cawley had suffered injuries and they bled, starving her body of oxygen. Her secondary cause of death, according to Dr Curtis, was postural asphyxia. She died because she couldn't breathe. If she had received prompt medical attention she probably would have lived. He told the jury that Dr Curtis had come to his conclusions without taking into account the blood spatters on the wall, without seeing the pool of blood on the decking and without seeing the injuries on Lillis himself. Mr Grehan reminded the jury

that the ambulance personnel who examined Lillis on that morning were all agreed that he was suffering from shock.

'If you were going to kill someone,' he said, looking up at the six men and six women, 'I suggest to you that you would do it properly.'

Anyone walking down the lane that morning could have seen what was happening on the patio, he pointed out, and if you were going to hit someone over the head to kill them you would not use moderate force. He turned to the subject of his client's labyrinthine lies. 'What a wicked web we weave,' he suggested. The lie had got out of control.

'He started on the lie, he continued on the lie, and he continued on the lie, it appears no matter what.'

Even when faced with his own clothing covered in his wife's blood, he clung to his lies. When asked about the mysterious note, which had, after all, been lying in plain view on the dressing table in his room, he continued to lie. He only stopped lying when he told his daughter and his former mistress almost a month after his wife's death.

The truth of what happened that day, Mr Grehan told the jury, was a lot more prosaic than the prosecution wanted them to believe.

'There was a row, and rows start over small things, the most innocent remark.'

He told the jury not to judge Lillis because he had been having an affair.

'Perhaps the strongest marriage, when you were totally fulfilled, can be rocked by a beautiful young woman, who has the capacity to roll back the years in terms of where your life is at. Who wouldn't be flattered', he asked them, 'when your hand is placed on the pulse of such a woman whose pulse you have caused to race.'

But, he said, that even if Lillis had reacted differently because of what was going on, it had still been a simple row with his wife.

'This is a court of law, not a court of morality, and you are not being asked to judge Mr Lillis's moral fibre.'

Lillis had lived fifty years without ever being in trouble, he pointed out. Even the gardaí agreed that no one they had spoken to had a bad word to say about him. He asked the jury to look long and hard at the prosecution case to see if they were convinced that Lillis had acted so out of character as to commit murder. If they had any doubt, they could not convict him. He ran through their options, through each of the four scenarios for manslaughter, ending each scenario with the reminder that this, too, would not be murder, but manslaughter. Of course, he reminded them, if they could find no reasonable reason to disbelieve Lillis's own account of what happened, they should acquit. The courtroom clock showed a couple of minutes before lunchtime.

'I'd ask you not to convict him,' he finished in a perfectly timed flourish, just as the timer showed 1 o'clock.

Justice White greeted the jury when they returned from lunch. The only task remaining before they began their deliberations was for him to summarise the evidence and to charge them with their duty. He was not here as either a sword for the prosecution or a shield for the defence, he told them, starting a brief preamble explaining once again the jury's role and the various options they would have to consider. Then he turned to the transcript in front of him. He did not intend to go over every single witness, he told the jury, just the main ones.

Eamonn Lillis looked almost grey as the tension of the case finally showed on his face. He bit his lip frequently as the judge highlighted the more damning pieces of evidence.

Justice White turned to the first day's evidence. He told the jury to cast their minds back to 12 January when they had heard Lillis's panicked call to the emergency services. This was the only direct evidence, apart from the account given by Lillis himself in court that Celine Cawley had been found on her side. He reminded the jury that they had heard the accounts of the paramedics who had arrived on the scene who had seen Lillis exhibiting all the symptoms of shock. He had been stumbling about and hadn't been making any sense. It was up to the jury, Justice White told them, to decide, 'Whether or not Mr Lillis was in shock or at what stage that shock might have occurred.'

He reminded them that Lillis had lied to the emergency services and to the gardaí throughout that day and had rung Detective Sergeant Kelly the following day to add to his story.

'What does this tell you about Mr Lillis and his ability to tell lies? So not only had Mr Lillis told the lie, he is now embellishing it the following day.'

Lillis had also lied in Howth garda station, the judge reminded them, when he told gardaí that the clothes he had on had been the same ones he was wearing when his wife sustained her injuries.

Justice White led the jury through the evidence given by Dr Haroon Kahn, who had examined Lillis at Howth garda station. The doctor had agreed that Lillis's injuries were consistent with a struggle, but had said that Lillis did not point out the injury to his ring finger. It had been in the doctor's notes, but no mention had been made in the consultation.

The judge reminded the jury that Lillis had given gardaí the name of a man who he blamed for the fictitious break in.

'It is a matter for you what inferences you draw that Mr Lillis is not alone perpetrating the lie but is now pointing the finger at an innocent man.'

Arriving at the point in the evidence when the contentious video footage of Rowan Hill had been shown, he commented that he had thought it in very bad taste and unnecessary.

Lillis stared at him intently when he talked about the notes found on the dressing table in Lillis's bedroom. Justice White told the jury:

'It is a matter for you – do you accept Mr Lillis's explanation for those notes, or do they have a more sinister meaning?'

He quoted the final line, 'You are running out of time' before moving on. Lillis had several opportunities to admit his lies, Justice White said. He quoted Lillis's protestations of innocence: 'I didn't kill her. I swear before God I couldn't do it to Celine.' In that same interview Lillis had denied having an affair, the judge said, glancing down at the pages of transcript in front of him. Even when asked directly about Jean Treacy, 'he seems to have played her position down.' When he was asked if they had a sexual relationship he had denied that as well and had dismissed the affair as 'perhaps being a mid-life crisis'. Justice White ran through the interviews, pausing occasionally to highlight the points where Lillis had lied or missed an opportunity to come clean. He quoted Lillis's continued denials, glancing up at the jury as he read the phrase, 'I haven't lied to you at all.'

'There again, ladies and gentlemen, you have the situation where Mr Lillis was being given yet another opportunity to cease the lie.'

He asked them to consider the phone traffic between Lillis and Jean Treacy. Did they think the increase in traffic in December compared to November significant?

'It is a matter for you, ladies and gentlemen, whether that indicated an increase of phone contact and whether that was consistent with a fling or whether it was beyond a fling at that stage.'

The court clock showed slightly after 4pm. Justice White looked down at both counsels. He had at least another hour of his charge to go. They would adjourn until tomorrow. The Cawley family at the back of the court looked dismayed that they would have to wait at least another day before any verdict would be announced.

The following morning, big crowds had gathered outside the courthouse for the conclusion of the case. Members of the court service sent most of the public back down four floors to the overspill room to watch proceedings on the large screens. Even without the dozens of onlookers, the court was crowded as the ranks of media had swelled with every day the verdict got closer. Silence fell as the court rose to their feet for the judge's entry and the jury filed in to take their seats.

Justice White picked up where he had left matters the previous evening. He continued to make comments as he went. After a few minutes he reached the evidence given by Jean Treacy. He neatly summed up the affair, saying of the pulse-feeling incident that it reminded him of the old song by Peter Sellers and Sophia Loren, 'Goodness Gracious Me' [in which Loren describes to her doctor (Sellers) how her pulse races every time he is near]. Shortly after this, he reached the account she had given of what Lillis had told her.

'Ms Treacy told you that Mr Lillis saw Ms Cawley fall. Mr Lillis said he didn't.' The judge whisked the jury through the daughter's evidence en route to the post-mortem testimony. Lillis put his hand up to his head as the judge once again outlined the manner of his wife's death. That done, all that was left was the testimony Lillis himself had given. Justice White gave a précis of the events of 15 December 2008 as told by Eamonn Lillis.

'It is up to you, ladies and gentlemen, what credibility you attach to having "a kiss and a cuddle" in circumstances when he was having a relationship with Ms Treacy.'

He ran through the rest of the account, pausing every now and then to comment on an inconsistency. Lillis had told gardaí he had walked the dogs as soon as he had returned from taking his daughter from school, but here in court he had said he had first done various domestic chores. Lillis had said the row was over putting out bird food and had described an exchange with Celine.

'Ask yourselves a question as to whether that was credible.'

A short time later another inconsistency: Lillis had been firm in court that he had seen very little blood on his wife's head. Justice White told the jury to compare that assertion with Ms Treacy's 'pool of blood'.

Justice White was known for his succinct summaries. Those familiar with his prowess in this regard were by now checking the clock, trying to work out how close the charge was to finishing and the jury deliberations beginning. He scanned the pages in front of him as he continued the story of the trial. He finished the evidence with Lillis's response to Mary Ellen Ring when she had asked him about what had happened on the morning of 15 December 2008. Lillis's reply, the judge said, was, 'I was there.'

He turned his attention to the prosecution and defence cases. The prosecution, he said, were saying Lillis was not credible:

'Mr Lillis is a man who just has no credibility. Who constantly lied to the Garda Síochána. Not only did he lie, but he sought to cast the blame on another individual.'

They had said of Lillis, 'He has no credibility, you can't

believe a word of what he said to you here in evidence, the same way you can't believe a word of what he said to the Garda Síochána.'

The prosecution case was for murder, and for murder there had to be an intent to kill or cause serious injury. The prosecution had said:

'The injuries observed by Dr Curtis are serious injuries. The natural and probable cause of blunt force trauma to the head is serious injury, and serious injury is there.'

The prosecution were saying that Lillis took an opportunity when it presented itself to him and that it was, 'All done with a clear, cool head. If there was any panic it only set in at a later stage, at the stage perhaps just before he phoned the emergency services, and they say that the truth of this case is that Mr Lillis murdered his wife.'

Turning now to the defence case, he told the jury that the defence were saying the state case was implausible and that it was ludicrous to suggest that Lillis would kill his wife in full view of the laneway passing by the bottom of the garden. The defence were saying that none of the injuries sustained by Celine Cawley in the row that morning were deliberately inflicted by Lillis. They admitted that Lillis had lied and continued lying, but he did so because he felt trapped.

'That is a matter for you, ladies and gentlemen, where the truth lies on this occasion.'

The summary finished, he turned now to the law of the case, and his charge began. He told the jury that if they thought Lillis's account was possibly true they must give him the benefit of the doubt and acquit. If they did not believe Lillis's account, then they must discount it and look at the remainder of the prosecution case to see if they could convict. He laid out the four options for manslaughter: self defence with excessive force, provocation, criminal negligence and failure of the prosecution to prove intent to murder. However, he warned the jury, Lillis himself had not put the case of self defence, provocation or negligence.

'It is a question for your consideration. Should you make the case for him if Mr Lillis doesn't make a particular case? Should you consider self defence? Should you consider provocation? Should you consider negligence?'

The charge had taken somewhat longer than the hour he had predicted the previous afternoon. Finally, with the clock approaching 12.45, he told the jury that they would now be given the issue paper. The single sheet of A4 containing the details of the charge and spaces for a verdict was handed to the foreman. They would be allowed to go for lunch before they started their deliberations, but once they were in their room, they must be kept together, even if one wanted a cigarette break and the rest were non-smokers. He told the jury that they were entitled to look at any piece of evidence and would have the transcripts of Lillis's interviews with the gardaí already. They could not have the book of evidence. Finally, he told them:

'Be prepared to talk. Be prepared to listen. Be prepared to have a view of the case. Be prepared to have that view altered.'

As the courtroom emptied for lunch, the chorus of 'Goodness Gracious Me' could be heard from various parts of the crowd old enough to remember the lyrics, as the press checked the details for their colour pieces:

'Boom boody-boom, boody-boom boody-boom,

Boody-boom, boody-boom, boody boom-boom-boom'

The crowd regrouped after lunch with an increased sense of anticipation. The wait was about to begin. At just before 2.30 the jury reassembled and then retired to their deliberations. When the door finally closed behind the last one, the registrar glanced up to check the clock. The jury had retired at 2.29 by the court clock, she announced. There was the briefest of silences, then the requisitions began. Requisitions are the submissions made by both prosecution and defence where they tell the judge what he missed out or even got wrong in this charge. They are normally quite brief.

Ms Ring stood up for the prosecution and informed Justice White that he had forgotten to tell the jury that they must reach a unanimous decision and also to agree on which option of manslaughter they were convicting, if that was the option they chose. The judge nodded and made a note before turning to the defence.

Mr Grehan got to his feet more slowly than usual. It seemed as if he was outraged beyond words. He glanced down at the notes in front of him before launching into his attack.

'Under our Constitution an accused under serious charges like this is entitled to trial by jury. We have an adversarial system where a judge is supposed to play the role of a judge of the law, not a director of the facts, not totally weighing matters against one party or another.'

The court listened with bated breath. The journalists who had begun roughing out their final accounts of the trial stopped tapping away on their laptops and reached for their notebooks. Mr Grehan was in full flow. The judge must be impartial, he said, the jury should know that the view of the prosecution was clearly theirs alone and the view of the defence was also a separate thing. There should be no third view. Mr Grehan reminded the judge that he had started his charge with the assertion that he was neither sword for the prosecution nor shield for the defence.

'I began to get very uneasy when you moved on to the evidence summary function in your charge.'

He stated, rather indignantly, that his fears had been

confirmed when it became clear that this was not going to be a blanket summary of the evidence.

'It was, in fact, a forensic dissection of the evidence with the aid of the entire transcript, to which you alone have access, which was directed to a total undermining of the defence.'

There was a ripple of concern around the room as the seriousness of his accusations became clear. He continued his tirade.

'I waited and waited and waited in vain for any balance to what the jury was being told.'

He told Justice White that his summary of the evidence had amounted to the selection of evidence that was damning to his client, as had his summary of the closing speeches. The whole thing, he said, was aimed at the jury bringing in a conviction of murder. The judge had suggested, Mr Grehan said, that Lillis's lies were evidence of his guilt. Even the highly partisan selection of evidence, the barrister continued, was 'twisted in a particular light'.

The judge's presentation of Dr Curtis's evidence had been one-sided and it had seemed that the other witnesses were all presented to be compared to the account given by the accused. Apart from all of this, the jury had not been given any assistance with how they were supposed to treat Lillis's many lies. In fact, they had been left with the impression that lies were a corroboration of guilt.

Justice White interrupted, frowning, 'I never made any such suggestion nor did I imply it.'

Mr Grehan barely paused for breath. Even when Justice White had finished summarising the evidence, he said, matters had not improved. When he had explained the law, he had managed to take back what he initially offered in the form of the different options for manslaughter. By saying that Lillis had not made the case for three of the options, he had left the jury thinking those options were no longer open to them. Then, finally, just as he was sending the jury out to start their deliberations, he had told them the book of evidence would not be available to them. Mr Grehan paused for effect. What could such a reference do other than make the jury think there was evidence they were not privy to that the judge had seen that led him to believe conviction was the only option?

'There is a real danger of the jury coming to that conclusion.'

Every single part of the evidence summary and the
charge had seemed to be undermining the defence case,
Mr Grehan said, and was driving the jury towards a
murder conviction.

'This is not something that can be fixed now. It cannot
be something that could be rebalanced by the court at
this stage. In fact, starting from scratch, you referred them
to matters in terms of omissions or slants being put on the
evidence they have heard, and in those circumstances I
feel I have no alternative but to ask the court to discharge
the jury.'

There was an attentive silence in the courtroom. All
around the room, people were holding their breaths. The
tension on the press benches was palpable … if the story
fell now at the final hurdle … images of blank pages and
massive rewrites swam in dozens of minds. Justice White
nodded at Mary Ellen Ring, who was already on her feet
to answer her colleague's accusations from the DPP's
viewpoint. Her colleague had talked about the respect

due to the jury system, she opened, part of that respect, surely, is also due to the intelligence of the jurors themselves. It was ridiculous to think that a judge would summarise every piece of evidence in a trial as complicated as a murder.

'Matters prosecution or defence hold dear are often not raised by the judge in summing up.'

The summary was, after all, exactly 'what it said on the tin': a concise account of the evidence of the trial. All matters had been touched on in this case, she said. It would be insulting the jury's good sense to prevent them from considering their verdict.

Justice White announced that he had no intention of discharging the jury at this stage in proceedings. The press benches heaved a united sigh of relief as the jury settled back into their seats a couple of minutes later. They had been deliberating for almost an hour at this stage but the additional charge they received now would put the clock back to zero for the official time of deliberations. Justice White smiled at them as they took their seats.

'I told you at the outset of my charge I did not carry a sword for the prosecution or a shield for the defence and I hope you don't think otherwise. I hope you don't think that my charge was directed at getting a particular verdict, because it was not.'

He had called them back, he said, to address certain matters where he was wrong in his initial charge. He set out the points that had been raised by both prosecution and defence. The defence had not simply been based on the unlikelihood of murder being committed in an open space. Neither were lies proof of guilt.

'People can lie for a myriad of reasons.'

The verdict of manslaughter was available to them under four different headings, he reiterated. Just because the accused man did not put the case himself did not mean the options were not open to them. However, if they went for a manslaughter verdict, he told them, they must all agree on the reason for their decision. He told the jury once again:

'I am here to give you directions on the law. I am here to assist you, but I am not here to impose my will on you or subtly point out the verdict I think you should return.'

Once again, the jury filed out of the room and the door closed behind them. It was now almost 3.30 by the court clock. At the cry of 'all rise' the court rose and watched the judge leave the room. The waiting had finally begun. People drifted away, looking for a cup of coffee or a smoke. The junior barristers' bench, located immediately in front of the first press bench, was suddenly cluttered with laptop chargers as the journalists made use of the banks of plug sockets that ran along the ledge in front of it. The cables snaked back to the row behind as the press tried to resuscitate dying batteries to get the final pieces written and ready to be filed as soon as the verdict was read out. The sweet papers began to accumulate in little piles along the pale wood of the seat.

But no sooner had people shifted in position to where they could read the papers in some degree of comfort on the hard wooden benches, than the door to the jury quarters opened. The jury manager emerged and hurried over to the bench where he had a whispered conversation with the registrar. After half an hour of deliberations, the jury had a question. The room filled back up quickly; people had not had time to go far. The Cawley family took their seats at the back of the court. Lillis was in his seat; his sisters were on the far side of the room with his small group of faithful friends.

After a couple of minutes, the judge came back from his chambers and the jury took their seats. The foreman leaned into the microphone on the desk in front of him. They wanted to see some of the evidence, he explained. He looked down at the note that contained a long and systematic list. They wanted a copy of the tape of the 999 call and a tape deck to play it on, the black plastic bag found in the attic, together with its contents, and the clothes found in the bedroom. They wanted the original garda statements given by both Lillis's daughter and Jean Treacy, and the transcripts for Lillis's testimony and that of Dr Curtis. He finished reading and sat back. There was a pause for a moment and a whispered conversation took place between the judge and the registrar. The more seasoned observers already knew that at least half the list was going to be refused.

Justice White smiled across at the jury members. The 999 call would be no problem, he said. These things were on DVD these days, but he had been assured that a method of playing it would be procured. There was no problem at all with the black plastic bag or the clothes found in the bedroom, they had already been admitted into evidence and so were available to the jury at any time. The garda statements were not so available. They had not made up part of the evidence and so would have to be denied. There was a similar problem with the transcripts, as they were not allowed for the jury. It was now just after 4.30 and he would have to make enquiries about where things stood. The jury would, therefore, be sent home for the night. There would be no verdict today.

The next morning, the crowd of onlookers had dwindled to a few diehards. The rest had decided that a day of waiting was not worth the hassle. For Lillis, the legal teams and the Cawley and Lillis families, there was no such luxury. Along with a press pack that was as big if not bigger than the attendance throughout the trial, they gathered to wait out the jury. The jury took their seats to be given the pieces of evidence they had asked for, and opted to listen back to Lillis's testimony, preferring to rely on their notes for the evidence of Dr Curtis. A short time later, Lillis's disembodied voice echoed over the courtroom, courtesy of the newly installed digital recording equipment that had replaced the traditional stenographers in the new courts. Once again, his voice could be heard recounting the details of his marriage and the death of his wife. The jury listened intently, their eyes closed in concentration. Lillis looked down at his notes, seemingly slightly uncomfortable at the recorded sound of his own voice. In the clarity of digital recording it sounded both like and unlike the voice of the man who had stood in the witness box only a couple of days before. His words, picked up by the microphone even when the ear had difficulty with his low, hurried delivery, were suddenly more nuanced than they had seemed on the day.

On the press benches the heads were bent. Some were working on final copy, others, like the jury, were listening intently to the disembodied voice. When the recording came to the description of finding his wife in a pool of blood on the patio, the voice, stripped of the visuals of reddening cheeks and welling eyes, sounded curiously detached. The jury had requested the evidence played up to the point that Lillis had dialled 999. His account had just got to the part where he explained that he could see no reason to worry about his wife's health, no reason why she would go from being OK to being unconscious, when the foreman spoke up. That was all they required.

They went back to their jury room, bringing with them with the means to play the 999 recording and the bag of bloody clothes. The door closed behind them and the waiting resumed. A little less than an hour later, they were called back to be sent to their lunch. They had only been deliberating for a little over an hour and a half by the reckoning of the court. By the afternoon the mixture of tension and tedium had lent a rather hysterical edge to the occasional laughter coming from the press benches. They almost had the court to themselves by now. Lillis and his sisters were nowhere to be seen and the Cawley family had retreated to the quiet of the Victim Support offices in another part of the complex. A debate was raging about whether the benches had been harder in the 200-year-old courtrooms of the recently vacated court-house or whether the new court held that dubious distinction. At 4.40 the jury manager appeared again and conferred with the registrar. The jury had succumbed to the lure of nicotine and were requiring a cigarette break.

The judge returned and announced his intention of sending them home as soon as possible. Juries were no longer sequestered overnight in a hotel if they failed to reach a decision in a day so they were frequently sent home earlier to allow both them and the judge a more relaxing evening. However, when this suggestion was put to the foreman, he shook his head. They would like to continue their deliberations that evening, he said. Speculation mounted that a decision might be close, and the press held their breath in anticipation of a verdict in time for the early evening news. But the clock ticked on and there was no sign of the jury manager, whose job it was to guard the jury and cater for their every request. At 5.30 Justice White appeared and announced that he was sending the jury home. Five minutes later, he did so. The jury had now been deliberating for almost four and a half hours in total. But for the families yet another day of waiting stretched ahead.

The next morning, Justice White waited until the jury had assembled. He looked down at them as they sat in their chairs, clutching their coats and bags as if itching to get back to their deliberations. They must wonder why they were brought into court every morning, he commented to them pleasantly, and why they were brought back every day before they went into lunch. The jurors stared back at him, a couple of them nodded slightly. It was because, he explained, he needed to know exactly how long they had been deliberating. Since the tally was now at approximately four and a half hours he was willing to accept a majority verdict from them from this point on. This would mean that at least ten of them should now agree on a verdict.

The jury left the courtroom and those that had gathered

quickly dispersed. The crowds of public were absent again today, but the journalists took up their stations beside the nearest plug sockets, their laptops open on their laps, surreptitiously watching the movements of the main players for the colour pieces later. Lillis had moved over to the glass wall that ran down one side of the new courthouse. He cast a lonely figure silhouetted in the watery winter sunlight, as he stared out at the Phoenix Park beyond. The Cawleys had walked out of the court in the opposite direction, seeking coffee and fresh air. The press and the gardaí clustered around the doors of the court, playing a cat and mouse game of deceptively idle conversation that hid some gentle probing. Neither side was fooled by the textbook responses. This trial was being handled by the book, even at this late stage there would be little or no official cooperation. Those garda who would comment would merely say that the trial was being carefully watched from the highest level. There would be no chance with this trial of a sneaky look at the book of evidence or an exclusive titbit not heard in court that could be used in the event of a guilty verdict.

The minutes passed by slowly and still there was no result. It had been expected, in as much as anything with juries can be expected, that once a majority verdict had been offered the verdict would be quick enough in coming, but the minutes turned into an hour and still there was silence from the jury room. Lunchtime came and went. Susanna Cawley took the opportunity to grab a few minutes' conversation with Lillis's younger sister, Carmel, in a secluded corner of the ground floor atrium. Throughout the trial the two families had never been less than civil to each other, but the strain of the long weeks of evidence had been hard on both. At just before four o'clock the jury manager finally made an appearance. People arrived as if from nowhere as the call went out that the jury were coming back, but the eagerness was short-lived.

The jury had a question. There was still no verdict. Looking tired and stressed, they took their seats and the foreman leaned into his microphone. They would like to take a break but when they came back could the judge run through the differences between the different verdicts one more time, he asked? They disappeared briefly and returned looking slightly more relaxed. Justice White patiently ran through the alternatives once again: the difference between murder and manslaughter, the four manslaughter options available and the possibility of acquittal. The jury listened carefully and took notes. When the judge was finished, the foreman looked at his fellow jurors enquiringly and conferred with the two closest jurors. Seeming satisfied, he nodded, and once again they retreated to their room. This time the courtroom didn't empty as quickly. Speculation was rife that such a question meant a verdict was near and no one wanted to risk missing the moment when it came. But one minute turned into ten, then half an hour, with no result. In the old courts, the jurors would knock on the panelled door that led to their room to signify their presence. The sound was one of the most electrifying noises there is. Jury waits would be spent on tenterhooks listening to every creak and rustle of the 200-year-old building. The new court had no such imperfections. The door of the jury room looked almost hermetically sealed and it certainly did not rattle even slightly in a passing breeze. The arrival of the jury manager and his polite whispering was a less impressive notification.

Despite that, when he did appear, soon after 6 o'clock, after almost nine and a half hours of deliberation, the anticipatory tension reached a peak. When the registrar gave the nod to indicate that this was indeed a verdict, mobile phones came flashing out of pockets to spread the news. The legal teams summoned their colleagues, the media alerted their newsrooms, others just passed on the impending news to anyone they thought would be interested. Lillis appeared and sat in his place, biting his lip furiously. Brendan Grehan arrived with a rustle of heavy black robes and Lillis dumbly watched his barrister sweep past to his seat. Across the courtroom his sisters took their customary seats, looking intensely nervous. The Cawley family came in a couple of minutes later and took their places in the back row of the middle bank of seats, glancing over at Lillis as they sat down. After what seemed like an eternity, the court rose as the judge took his place. Then, finally, the jury filed into the room, occupying the same seats they had sat in every day of the trial. They looked extremely serious. Several of the women were in tears. The registrar stood and addressed them.

'Have you reached a verdict on which at least ten of you are agreed?'

The foreman replied that they had.

'Have you recorded the verdict on the issue paper?'

They had.

The registrar crossed to take the folded paper and returned to her seat. Lillis stood up and stared straight ahead. The registrar showed the paper to the judge, then turned to face Lillis.

'The accused is guilty of manslaughter.'

Lillis did not react, but his face reddened. The registrar continued reading from the issue paper. The tension clearly visible on the jurors' faces showed just how difficult their decision had been. In the end it was one on which ten of them had agreed. Faced with so many different possibilities, the foreman had helpfully added in the reason for their decision. They had gone for the fourth manslaughter option: that intent to murder had not been proven. Lillis tilted his chin up in a nervously defiant gesture. Across the room, his sisters seemed to sag slightly with relief – it could have been so much worse. At the back of the silent courtroom Celine's niece, Joanna, burst into tears and was comforted by her father, Chris Cawley. Celine's sister, Susanna, was holding herself together with difficulty in the face of the intrusive glances from the press a few rows in front of her.

Ms Ring asked for the sentence to be deferred to allow the Cawley family time to prepare a victim impact statement. Mr Grehan quickly asked that his client be allowed out on bail until sentencing to get his affairs in order before he was sent to prison. Justice White agreed, setting the sentence date for six days' time. However, he reminded the still standing Lillis that he was not now an accused man on remand, but a convict. He would have to sign on twice daily at Howth garda station until his sentencing. The press carefully noted the daily times of between nine and twelve in the morning and six and nine in the evening. They would be waiting.

Justice White thanked the jury for their care and attention in judging the case and excused them from further jury service for life. Their part was now over, he told them, but if they chose to attend the sentence the following Thursday he would be glad to see them in the crowd that would no doubt gather and they would be welcome to sit in the seats they had occupied throughout the trial. With that, it was over. The court slowly emptied. Finally, Susanna Cawley's resolve broke and the tears streamed down her face as she passed by the crowds of media clustered around the doors of the court. The press milled about anxiously, looking for someone who might give them a quote.

Eventually the news filtered through that the Cawley family intended to say a few words once they had had time to compose themselves. The journalists made their way down to the front of the building where the photographers were already waiting en masse. The sea of cameras surged forward every time the automatic doors opened, with the journalists pushing to the front. Each time, they fell back, disappointed, after giving a hapless tracksuit-wearing client of the district courts an inflated sense of their own importance. Tension was high as everyone was focused on his or her deadline. On one of the surges, two photographers snapped and turned on each other, to be pulled apart with much swearing.

Then the shout went up that Lillis had been seen entering the central atrium. He came striding out of the building, his head down and his hands plunged deep into the pockets of his sombre black coat. He ignored the microphones that were thrust in his face and the questions shouted at him by the hopeful journalists. He simply pushed through the throng and made his way to the black car waiting at the side of the road a few feet away. The photographers raced after him, knocking any parked bikes flying in their eagerness not to miss the perfect shot. Lillis ignored them totally, and got into the car as the flashes flared in his face. The face of his daughter could be seen palely illuminated in the driver's seat beside him before the car quickly sped away into the evening.

The photographers drifted back to the doors of the courthouse and the waiting continued. Eventually, the

Cawley family could be seen coming down the curved staircase at the back of the atrium. They stood for a moment at the bottom as if steeling themselves for the onslaught. Then, as a group, they came forward. As the doors opened to release them the press surged forward and the snapping of shutters was almost deafening. Chris Cawley stepped forward to announce that there would be no comment until the sentence had been handed down the following week, and then he and his family moved to leave. The photographers followed them in a wave, forcing them to stop for one last photograph on the steps of the courthouse before they were finally allowed to depart to deal with the news in something approaching peace.

CHAPTER 9

Aftermath

The following morning, at around 10 o'clock, Eamonn Lillis arrived to sign on at Howth garda station. He was greeted by a mass of photographers and journalists who had been camped out, waiting for his arrival. It would be the first time this ritual was played out but it certainly would not be the last. For the six days he was on bail he was followed constantly by a posse of photographers. Each time he appeared to sign on, there were journalists waiting to comment on his choice of outfit, and the fact that he was still driving the same black, four wheel drive Mercedes ML in which he had conducted his furtive meetings with Jean Treacy.

The photographers were ever present. They followed him to the stables when he went to watch his daughter ride for one last time. They followed him to the local shop when he went to pick up peat briquettes. The following day, the papers were full of headlines about the killer revisiting the Summit shop where he had bought the newspaper on the morning of his crime. Photographers maintained a constant presence down the laneway beside Rowan Hill, hoping for a shot of someone on the decking where Celine had died. They even climbed into the overhanging branches of nearby trees to try and get the perfect shot. By some unknown means, the laneway was now littered with dog faeces, in an obvious protest at their intrusion into the privacy of this leafy road.

In Swords, the house that Jean Treacy was once again sharing with the all-forgiving Keith was also being staked out, as it had been since her appearance in court and non-appearance in front of the photographers. A picture of her, taken at a party, staring red-eyed into the camera, had been smiling out of almost every paper since the first photos appeared in the weekend papers after her appearance. Stories were circulating on the Internet about journalists handing out cards in the newsagents near her parents' home in Tipperary to surprised passersby. She was seen as both the innocent prey of the ravening hordes of media and as a manipulator of the powers-that-be. Her wish for privacy when she gave evidence had become a national news story. Politicians, including Labour Senator Ivana Bacik and Socialist Party MEP Joe Higgins, both discussed the matter on their blogs. In the *Irish Independent,* senior barrister Michael O'Higgins SC commented on the setting of a dangerous precedent. He told the paper that while he could understand that Ms Treacy had been in an intensely embarrassing situation, he would be worried, as a criminal defence barrister, if the matter became common practice.

'But in a different case, in a different situation, a witness could be told that they were going to be a State witness one way or the other – the easy way or the hard way. They could be told that gardaí would do their best to protect them from the media.

'In those circumstances there might be a temptation (on the part of the witness) to sugar-coat their statement because they are dealing with gardaí who could be in a position to help them out.'

Meanwhile, as her treatment was being debated around the country, Ms Treacy had retreated to the home of her brother in Northern Ireland. Despite this, the stakeout outside the Swords house continued. Everyone who had played a part in the unfolding story of the trial was bombarded with requests from the press. Stephen Larkin, the innocent man on whom Lillis had sought to place the blame, was tracked down and photographed, and multiple papers carried the story that his privacy had been destroyed and that he would like to sue Lillis for falsely pointing the finger. In an interview in January 2010 he said that the false accusation had caused him to become ill and depressed. He had been 'suicidal', seeing 'no more point in living' and had had to have in-patient therapy. He was still on anti-depressants, he said.

The newspaper coverage in the days that followed the conviction was blanket. No aspect of the case or the lives of those at its centre went unexplored. Even the CCTV footage from the newsagent's shop, which recorded Lillis's visit on the morning of the killing, appeared on front pages. The newspapers saw their sales rise as the public lapped up every lurid detail.

But the case was generating more than column inches. By the following Monday, the papers were reporting that the Garda Commissioner, Fachtna Murphy, was to meet representatives of the press body, National Newspapers of Ireland, to discuss the special treatment Jean Treacy had received. The matter had already been widely argued during the trial in the wake of the actual event, but now it gained even greater legitimacy by becoming a political issue. Commissioner Murphy let it be known that he fully supported the decision to shield Ms Treacy from view, and he was backed by the Minister for Justice, Dermot Ahern, who commented that the move may have been made to ensure her co-operation, sparking another volley of indignation on the Internet where, in forums, on blogs and on social networking sites like Twitter, the debate had been raging ever since Ms Treacy had taken the stand. The matter even ended up being raised in the Seanad, and at each level there were more mutterings about privacy legislation and press intrusion.

Ever since the hysteria that surrounded the Joe O'Reilly

trial, when the thirty-five-year-old advertising executive, who was subsequently convicted of killing his wife, had vehemently denied his involvement to a variety of journalists and even to the nation on his celebrated appearance on the 'Late Late Show', certain trials attracted a lot of scrutiny. Although it was widely accepted in press circles that the Lillis trial was a completely different kind of story to that of a cold-blooded killer like O'Reilly, it still had the seductive whiff of sex, money and intrigue. For each of the six days that separated his conviction from his sentence, Lillis made the front pages. Sharing the limelight each time his name was splashed across the front page of one of the tabloids was Ms Treacy, whose picture would feature beside Celine's and those of the Cawley family, on an almost daily basis.

Each day there was another picture of Lillis signing on at Howth garda station and each day there was further coverage. Even though, legally, the case was still live until the sentencing, and therefore the press coverage still needed to be reasonably circumspect, the media contented themselves with the news they could cover.

There had already been several 'souvenir' inserts with a comprehensive wrap-up of all the main points of evidence in the trial, and still the hungry public continued to buy the papers. Eamonn Lillis had become one of an elite band of convicts whose name could guarantee a spike in sales. The dubious honour would, in all likelihood, be with him for life.

By the time the day of the sentencing arrived, almost every aspect of his daily life had been catalogued and photographed. At least during the trial the attention had been centred on one far from ordinary day. By the Wednesday of that week the victim support group Advocates for Victims of Homicide (Advic) had voiced their displeasure that a convicted killer should be allowed out on bail. They called on the government to introduce legislation to prevent convicted criminals having the 'luxury of freedom' before they were sentenced.

Finally, on 4 February 2010, not quite a month after his trial had started, the crowds gathered one last time for the show as the court convened for Eamonn Lillis's sentencing, while the morning headlines reported on his last meal with his daughter.

Justice White was by now already engaged with another trial, so proceedings had moved with him to a different court. The crowd assembled on the second floor long before the scheduled 10.30am start. Once again, the regular onlookers had arrived in force; the same familiar faces that appear in the public gallery of any high profile trial. They were joined by friends and neighbours who had come to show their support to the Cawley family, and a few who had come to show their support for Eamonn Lillis. This morning, however, the crush that had filled the courtroom every day of the trial was eased as the majority of the public were sent downstairs to the viewing room down there. The press were allowed in and swarmed to take their seats. Lillis's sister, Carmel, took her seat, as she had every day in the other court-room, in the second row behind the jury box. Elaine, her older sister, sat stiffly beside her, and next to her sat Lillis's college friends, Gerry Kennedy and Siobhan Cassidy. Across the room from them, in their customary seats at the back of the court, were the Cawley family, sitting tensely as they waited for the day to begin.

At 10.45 Justice White took his seat. Sergeant Gary Kelly took the stand and was led through the facts of the case by Mary Ellen Ring. The familiar details of the morning of 15 December were run through, then the post mortem and Lillis's interviews with gardaí. She finished with the principal dates of both Lillis's and Celine's lives. Birthdays, marriage, the birth of their daughter, the setting up of Toytown Films. Lillis had no previous convictions, she noted, and had never expressed remorse about the death of his wife to either gardaí or the Cawley family. She sat down and Mr Grehan got to his feet.

He, too, concentrated on the biographical details. His client was fifty-two years old, he confirmed with Sgt Kelly, and before the matter before the court now, had never come to the attention of gardaí in any way. Sgt Kelly agreed that Lillis had been described as someone who wouldn't hurt a fly and who had been visibly shaking and in shock when emergency services arrived to attend to his wife. The gardaí had always had their eye on Lillis in the matter of his wife's death, Mr Grehan suggested. They had put some very provocative questions to him in interview? Sergeant Kelly shook his head. Mr Grehan pursued his point.

'I am suggesting gardaí were provocative in asking questions.'

Sgt Kelly shook his head. They had been 'determined, not provocative'.

'Do you agree that the gardaí were provocative?'

'I wouldn't say provocative.'

The sergeant stubbornly dismissed any suggestion of heavy-handed questioning. Mr Grehan moved his attention to the media. Sgt Kelly confirmed that the media had maintained a constant presence at Rowan Hill since Lillis had been convicted. It had even been necessary to call the gardaí on a number of occasions. Mr Grehan described photographers up stepladders and in the trees, doing everything in their power to get shots of Lillis at home. They had followed Lillis and his daughter to the stables, he said, and had followed Lillis into town. They were there every time he went to sign on at Howth garda station. There was no reaction from the press benches;

the journalists were all bent over their notebooks, being careful not to miss a single syllable. Mr Grehan continued his attack. The photographers had even, he said, with a show of righteous indignation, at times made inflammatory remarks to try and get a reaction out of his client. Sgt Kelly couldn't confirm that but added:

'I did see them chase him up the road.'

Justice White leaned forward to question the sergeant. He immediately pulled matters back to Lillis's failure to own up to his actions. Had Lillis agreed with any proposition put to him? he asked Sgt Kelly. The sergeant confirmed that Lillis had not changed his story once during the investigation. Justice White turned his attention to the dramatic admissions at the start of the trial [that there was 'no burglar in the home, no intruder or other party present other than the accused himself on the occasion when Celine Cawley suffered the injuries that resulted in her death.'] Had they actually been of any practical use to the prosecution, or were they all matters that would have been proven in the course of the trial anyway? The garda did not answer. The court had heard much of the prosecution's proof that the intruder story was a fabrication, evidence introduced despite these admissions, as proof of Lillis's capacity to lie. The judge didn't comment further and Sgt Kelly's role was at an end.

He stepped down from the witness box, and Ms Ring stood up once more. There were two victim impact statements, she said, from Susanna Cawley [Coonan] and from Celine's daughter. Neither was to take the stand, she explained. In fact, the daughter's statement would not even be read out in open court. However, she would read the statement on behalf of the Cawley family, written by Celine's sister, Susanna. Ms Ring looked down at the typewritten pages in her hand and started reading, so quickly that even the most vigilant note-takers had difficulty keeping up.

'It's next to impossible to put into words what has happened in our lives since December 15th 2008,' began Susanna's statement. 'However, I will do my best.'

'The good humoured, roguish, fun, compassionate sister has been utterly deleted from my mind and replaced with the horror of blood and the shaven-headed dead body.'

It was the image of her sister 'slipping in blood and frost and fighting for her life on the patio of the house of her dreams' that had stuck in her mind, she wrote.

'It is the not knowing that is the really haunting part of it.'

Ms Coonan had written that she had been with both her sister Barbara and her mother when they had passed away from cancer, and that their deaths had been a 'triumph over illness'.

'For Celine and those of us who mourn her deeply we were utterly deprived of any dignity, spirituality or peace in her passing ... Even her funeral was a media circus, bereft of the usual ritual and comfort.'

She wrote that Lillis's lies had robbed her family of the truth about Celine's death.

'The endless lies and scenarios are all in my mind right now and that terrifying realisation that I will probably never really know what happened. At night I play the scenes over and over in my head. Was she in pain? Was she conscious? Did she think of [her daughter]? Did she know she was dying? There is one person who knows the answers to all of these questions, but it seems I will never know and that's hard to accept. It was a terrifying realisation that I will probably never know what happened on December 15th.'

Even once Lillis had been charged, she wrote, they were told almost nothing. As the trial had approached and there was a danger of prejudicing it, they had had to walk a legal tightrope. They still walked one for the sake of Celine's daughter. Ms Coonan, a solicitor like her husband and her father, wrote about the legal vacuum in which they found themselves in trying to provide for Celine's child. They had no *locus standi* – a legal term meaning they had no right to be heard – she said, and had experienced major difficulties trying to make financial and residential arrangements for the girl. Ms Coonan wrote that if it had been she who had died, her sister would have been 'sorting out' her three children. She said that even though she had felt a strong moral obligation to help there was no opening given 'even to assist'.

'I think Celine would have been cross with me for

standing by politely.'

Her sister, she wrote, was always 'happy to muck in'. She had been such a generous godmother and aunt.

'She would know all their birthdays and brought age appropriate presents. She was a big kid herself and probably got as much from the remote control tractors and fluffy puppies as the kids.'

But the happy memories were short-lived, and the statement soon drifted back to Lillis's fabrications.

'The treacherous lies are overwhelming. The worst had to be the one told to us by Eamonn of the intruder and Celine's last moments.'

Lillis had particularly betrayed the trust of the 'wonderful, honourable man, my eighty-year-old dad.' James Cawley put his hand to his face as his daughter's angry words were read out.

'Whatever about the rest of us, Dad deserves to know the truth.'

Susanna's statement continued, attacking her brother-in-law's failure to come clean:

'Lack of remorse is hard to credit. He had thirteen

months' opportunity to at least apologise to [his daughter] and my father. No such apology was forthcoming.'

As if forcing herself to turn away from the open wound of the betrayal, Ms Coonan once again described the sister she had known. A vibrant force who had found a channel for her drive and organisational skills in production, and once there, had gone from strength to strength. Her sister, she wrote, 'put a stamp on people's hearts'. She paid tribute to all the friends and acquaintances who had shown their support in the crowds who attended the trial. Even Celine's old maths teacher had come along in the first week. She remembered particularly Celine's best friend and cousin, Juliette Hussey, 'who is still devastated and whose life was also shattered.' Ms Coonan thanked the garda team who had conducted the investigation, telling them they would have a place ensured in heaven.

'You can bet Celine has put St Peter out of a job manning the gates of heaven.'

Finally, addressing her sister, she wrote: 'our lives are enriched for knowing you', then a quote from the Take That song, 'Rule the World' that had featured so movingly at Celine's funeral.

'*All the stars are out tonight.*

They're lighting up the sky tonight for you.'

The Cawley family were in tears. Even Lillis looked red-faced as he listened. As she read the final line, Ms Ring's voice cracked with surprising emotion.

'We still and we will always miss you desperately. We shall struggle on. Thank God for having known you.'

Ms Ring sat down and bent her head over her notes. There was a brief silence before Mr Grehan got to his feet. He had several character witnesses to speak on Lillis's behalf, he told the judge. A man who had been sitting beside Lillis's sisters behind the jury box stood up and made his way over. Gerry Kennedy, the same man who had provided a surety of €50,000 for Lillis when he was released on bail back in early January 2009, was a familiar face to those who had attended the trial regularly. He could often be seen during the trial, in deep conversation with Lillis, and always sat with the accused man's sisters. He had been vocal in his disapproval of the crush outside the court each morning which his friend had to push through to meet his legal team.

Mr Kennedy told the judge that he had known Lillis since 1975 when they were in UCD together. They had been friends for almost thirty-five years and he counted Lillis as one of his closest friends.

'A gentleman, kind, considerate and a very, very good listener.'

He said that when his brother was killed in a car crash in Mexico in 1980, Lillis had been a tremendous support to both him and his family and that this would never be forgotten. Lillis had been the only man he had wanted to be godfather for his daughter, he said, and he had been an 'absolute champion' in that regard. When Lillis and Celine had their daughter, they had asked him to be her godfather.

'It was a fantastic honour to be asked.'

Over the years they had worked together quite a bit. They were both advertising copywriters by trade. Mr Kennedy said that he knew his friend missed his wife.

'He misses Celine a lot; certainly in conversation he would do anything to have her back.'

He said that Lillis was 'almost the last person in the world I would have felt would have been here today.'

He was not just saying this because Lillis was an old friend, he emphasised, he was a gentleman.

'I believe he was then and I believe he still is.'

Mr Kennedy stepped down and hurried back to his seat past his old friend. His place was taken by another college friend, Siobhan Cassidy. She had known Lillis for thirty-four years, she said, having also met him while studying English in UCD. She had always found him to be a 'mild mannered' man, 'very gentle and very courteous, and my opinion of him has never changed'.

Mr Grehan asked her if she had ever seen Lillis be confrontational. No, came the rather indignant response.

'He was the opposite, quite non confrontational,' she said. 'He was interested in the human spirit, film and poetry.'

She had also asked Lillis to be the godfather to her first born child, and he had been wonderful.

'He has never failed her on any occasion in her life.'

She said the love between Lillis and his daughter was

obvious. She had remarked to her husband when she had first heard about Celine's death 'Thank God [their daughter] has him.'

She got down from the stand and Mr Grehan announced that he now had a few brief submissions on behalf of his client. Finally, after thirteen months where no private apology was forthcoming, the Cawley family received one given in the full glare of the media. Lillis said he was 'extremely sorry and regretful' for what had happened and would always love his wife. He had loved his wife very much, Mr Grehan told the court, and he would love her for the rest of his life – he still talked about her in the present sense. She had been partner 'in every sense of the word'. Sitting dumbly on his bench, his words read by his counsel, Lillis said that, contrary to reports, his wife was 'neither a bully nor a tyrant'. Celine had been a 'loving mother and wife as well as a strong and talented businesswoman'.

Lillis's thoughts were now with his daughter, Mr Grehan said.

'They have a very close and loving relationship. She is

the only part of Celine left in his life.'

Lillis was 'fearful of the consequences of his actions for her now and in the future' his barrister continued.

He was 'extremely sorry and regretful for what happened and for his subsequent behaviour, in particular the lies he told, in particular to Celine Cawley's family'.

Mr Grehan said to Justice White that, having regard to the jury's unusually clarified verdict, his client should be sentenced according to the guidelines for involuntary manslaughter. The jury had found that the prosecution had failed to prove intent, and the sentence should reflect that. Apart from that, he said, the trial had generated an unusual amount of press attention and he had no doubt that it would continue to do so. He told the judge that when someone had been photographed and named to the extent that Lillis had, he could suffer the additional punishment of becoming a pariah in his own society. It was unlikely that his client would ever be able to continue a normal life even after he had served his time in jail. This should also be taken into account in the matter of sentencing. Finally, he said, account should be taken of the daughter, 'the centre-most victim in this'. He would not seek to use her as a 'crutch', he said, but his client was now the sole parent of his daughter and so he was looking for the judge's sympathy in that regard. With that, he finished putting his case and it was now the turn of the prosecution.

The DPP took a very dim view of pointing the finger at an innocent man, Ms Ring said. The fact that Eamonn Lillis had actually named someone as a suspect was taken very seriously and was definitely an aggravating factor. She also advised the judge to consider the 'disregard' Lillis had shown his wife when she was lying injured. He had not even called out to her. She confirmed that Lillis had never offered to plead guilty of manslaughter and that the moderate force used in the injuries would not have been accidental. The term 'involuntary manslaughter' she said was a misleading term and the DPP would regard this case as one on the upper end of the manslaughter scale. She told Justice White that the Cawley family would provide for Lillis's daughter regardless of what may or may not have been put in place for her. She would soon be eighteen and so would have a say in her own future. Finally, turning to the matter of the media attention, she said that no one had any control over the publicity but Lillis might have legal options available to him in the future. Besides, the publicity was a direct result of his actions.

Justice White deferred the case until the morning, saying he needed time to read through the various reports and the two victim impact statements. He remanded Lillis overnight in Cloverhill Prison. Lillis looked shocked as he was led away by several prison officers.

The following morning, the *Evening Herald* was first with the news that Lillis had spent a 'restless and tearful night' in a solitary cell under 'special observation'. In the next day's papers he would be known by his prison number, but for now all eyes were on another number, that of the years he would serve. As the crowd gathered outside the doors of the court for one last time, speculation was rife. The members of the public who were regular attendees at high profile trials stood discussing sentencing practice with the air of seasoned barristers. A few feet away from them, the journalists were engaged in a similar discussion, trying to work out which past sentences were fair comparisons. Eventually the doors opened to admit the press. They streamed into the front seats in a well practised wave. All but the most determined members of the public were sent down to the ground floor to watch the sentencing on the big screens. A few minutes later, Lillis's supporters came to take their customary seats. His sister Carmel sat, as always, on the end of the row, but today her sister was absent. She had been unable to reschedule her flight back to the UK and so had had to go and reclaim her normal life. Today the ever faithful Gerry Kennedy sat beside Carmel. The Cawley family came in at a few minutes to 11. Before he took his seat, James Cawley crossed the short distance that separated his family's seats from the Lillis camp. He bent to talk to Carmel and gave her a hug before retreating back to his seat. The waiting had been hard on everyone.

When Lillis came through the door that led to the

downstairs cells, their eyes swivelled towards him. He looked pale and drawn after his first night in a cell as a convict. He sat down and spoke to one of the prison officers who had come in with him, nodding over towards his sister and his friends. There was a whispered conversation before the guards retired. Lillis gestured to Mr Kennedy to go over to him. He looked annoyed. He had been told he could talk only to one of them. His friend went back over and murmured the news to Carmel who promptly got up and went to speak to her brother. She stayed with him until the judge arrived at almost 11.10.

When Justice Barry White had taken his seat and the body of the court had resumed theirs, Lillis stood up to hear his fate. Justice White looked down at him with a very serious expression on his face.

'Mr Lillis, the jury have found you guilty of manslaughter.'

He told Lillis that the reason for the verdict that the foreman had written on the issue paper made it clear that they rejected Lillis's contention that he had nothing to do with his wife's death and had decided that her death had indeed been unlawful. He said that the sentence for man-slaughter could be anything from a suspended sentence to life in prison, and he had carefully considered what the appropriate sentence should be. The defence would say that this case was at the bottom end of the spectrum, while the prosecution were of the exact opposite view. It was up to him whether either of them was right. To make his decision he had returned to the evidence put before the jury.

'That evidence disclosed that, having injured your wife, at least you had the decency to phone the emergency services and, as far as I can see, that is the only decent act or acts you committed on that particular morning.'

He said that the actions Lillis had engaged in before he made that call had been for the sole reason of covering up his involvement, the same reason that lay behind the continuous lies. He had only relinquished those lies after he had been charged, when he gave an account to his daughter and to Jean Treacy. Taking all the facts of the case into account, and looking at the sentences that had been passed on previous occasions, he considered the correct term for Lillis's crime to be ten years. He would also, however, have to take into account any mitigating and aggravating factors. He had read both victim impact statements handed into him the day before and it was clear what a devastating effect Lillis's actions had had, right across the generations, from his eighty-year-old father-in-law to his seventeen-year-old daughter. He referred back to Susanna Coonan's statement and her description of her father as gentlemanly. He said he had observed Mr Cawley himself throughout the course of the trial, and he had 'no doubt there is not a single word of exaggeration' in the victim impact report before him. He then turned to the daughter's statement.

'It sets out how she has changed from a sixteen-year-old girl into a hardened seventeen-year-old adult.'

He informed Lillis that the impact on all between these two extremes was obvious. He had taken account of the fact that Lillis was a fifty-two-year-old man, he said, and that the offence had been out of character, although he found it hard to reconcile this mild- mannered man with the description Lillis himself had given of saying to his wife that she could shove the brick 'where the sun didn't shine'. He considered Lillis's expression of remorse to be self-serving in the light of all the circumstances of the case. Lillis had not offered a plea of manslaughter and he considered the admissions made at the start of the trial to be of no assistance to the case. Finally he turned his attention to the press coverage.

'This case has attracted considerable media interest and public attention. I am conscious that on your release from prison you will still or are likely to be still of interest to the media, and I am taking that into account in impos-ing sentence on you.'

On this note he announced that he was reducing the sentence by three years, to one of seven years. There was silence in the courtroom.

Justice White continued talking.

'In considering the victim impact reports I have received and heard in this case, it seems to me the media have little or no respect for the privacy or dignity of the Cawley family. It is also clear to me from watching news bulletins that there has been a constant media scrum whenever you entered or left this building. I consider that to be an affront to human dignity.'

The journalists took down his words, glancing surreptitiously around the courtroom to see the reactions from the two families. There was none. Justice White continued that he had heard from Lillis's daughter's statement and from Sergeant Kelly's evidence the way in which his daughter had been hounded by the media.

'I can but request that that ceases and call on the media to respect the privacy of the Cawley family.'

There was a brief silence. Mr Grehan stood up and formally asked for leave to appeal. The judge formally refused him, the standard legal response for such a request. Lillis would now have a fortnight to lodge an application for leave to appeal. Chris Cawley's wife, Sorcha, got up and left the courtroom, visibly upset, her husband following close behind her. As they left the room, the judge reduced Lillis's sentence by a further month to account for the time he had served in jail while he was on remand. Finally it was all over.

Once Justice White had left the courtroom, everyone

stood up and began milling around. Lillis was led away, back to the cells and the press gathered into groups, waiting for the next development. James Cawley crossed the room to Lillis's sister Carmel and gave her a warm hug. Susanna came over and also gave Carmel a hug. A small, folded piece of paper passed between them. The relief of both families that their shared ordeal at such a public trial was at an end was obvious, whatever they might separately think of the sentence. James Cawley was in conversation with Superintendent David Dowling who had been overseeing the case. He was heard to say to him, 'thank God it is all over now.' The court was emptying slowly. The Lillis party walked past the crowd of press gathered outside the courtroom with polite refusals to comment. They made their way round to the canteen and disappeared off to a quiet table. The Cawleys vanished into the victim support offices and the press were left standing uncertainly about, or talking animatedly into their phones, relaying the best lines from the morning's proceedings. Soon word came back that the Cawley family would make a brief statement outside, and the pack moved down to the front steps. Once again, there were dozens of photographers waiting outside and the journalists immediately stood in front with their microphones, to the displeasure of the photographers.

After the mayhem that had occurred outside the court after the verdict was announced, it was decided that the photographers should be allowed to take their shots first before the journalists could move in for their quotes. When the Cawley family finally came through the double doors, they were met by a barrage of lenses, but the reporters hung back. Once the fluttering of the shutters had finally come to a close, the journalists moved in, and, afraid of missing the perfect shot, the photographers surged forward again around them. There were some shouts and then order was briefly restored.

Chris Cawley stepped forward to read a prepared statement. He thanked everyone who had stood with them through the trial and the gardaí who had conducted the investigation. The strain of the past three weeks on him became all too evident and his brother-in-law, Andrew Coonan, stepped forward to continue the thanks, then

Chris stepped in again to talk about his sister. His voice broke as he described Celine as a 'dynamic, kind, successful, fun loving, caring person.'

'She had a beautiful energy that lit up so many lives ... we love you, Celine.'

When it became clear that there was no more to be said, the reporters fell back and were replaced by the crowd of photographers, who followed the Cawleys to the steps of the courthouse. The family paused with quiet dignity as the photographers arranged themselves below them, posing for one last united shot that would appear on the front page of every paper the next day.

Before most copy had been filed, the sentence was already being discussed over the airwaves. RTÉ's 'Joe Duffy Show' devoted a segment to the breaking news and the listening public were not shy of having their say on the matter. The overwhelming view was that Justice White's sentence had been far too lenient. Many had taken exception to the jury's verdict, and the facts of the case were dissected by those who had gleaned their information from plentiful sources in the newspapers.

They spoke as if they knew the Cawley family and stoutly defended their honour and the reputation of Celine herself. The trial had become a pool for every form of gender stereotyping and the age-old battle of the sexes. In the eyes of many who commented, it was as if it was no longer about two people in a marriage but about male/female stereotypes. They bayed for Lillis's blood, partly because he had been branded a weak man. On the Internet, the comment was just as fierce. Forums and blogs were discussing the news of the sentence within minutes of it being delivered. The micro blogging site Twitter, where many had been watching the tweets coming from the court itself, was alive with chatter about the validity of the verdict and the sense of the sentence.

The papers on the following day, all of whom found a way to refer to Lillis's prison number in their accounts, were full of criticism of the sentence, with many pointing out that, with the automatic reduction of sentencing by one quarter available to all prisoners, Lillis would be likely to serve only five years. By Sunday, the media had turned a large portion of their attention to themselves.

The coverage of the case was pored over by a host of columnists and commentators who were highly critical of their colleagues. Michael Clifford, who had attended the trial himself for the paper, writing in the *Sunday Tribune*, said:

'While there is an argument that the coverage was again reflecting public interest, any notion of taste and boundaries seems to have been abandoned. Demented competition has ensured that the coverage for a trial of this nature is in danger of descending into frenzy. The media business might well take heed of the excesses as described by the various parties last week. If ever politicians were looking for an excuse to push through a privacy bill – designed largely to protect the powerful from legitimate inquiry – the Lillis trial has provided them with further fodder.'

In the *Sunday Independent*, reporter Jody Corcoran, who had also been among the throngs of press attending the trial, wrote an opinion piece under the headline 'Why We Should Be Glad the Media Cannot Act as Judge and Jury', in which he assessed the media coverage of Justice

White's comments at the sentencing. He observed the outrage in the press that had followed the sentence, and commented:

'But it is not for a media group, in my opinion, to dispense what a team of editorial executives may decide is justice when such a decision proves to be a significant factor in a reduction of a prison term which a judge may deem appropriate – only for that media group to then decry as an "insult" the reduced sentence imposed.'

Undeterred, the media continued their fascination with Lillis. He had now become one of an elite band of criminals whose name could be guaranteed to increase sales. In the days that followed his sentencing, the papers investigated every aspect of his prison life. He made the front page when he was allotted a job in jail; it seemed particularly fitting to those writing that this job should happen to be in the prison print shop. The few words he had exchanged with a journalist waiting outside Howth garda station on one of his signing-on visits was now presented as his only interview. He had answered a question about how he felt about going to jail. It was his biggest fear, he had responded. Other sources spoke of his surprise at the severity of his sentence. In contrast with the vocal public objections to the perceived shortness of the sentence, he was apparently taken aback by the length of time stretching ahead of him and was looking ahead to his spell in jail with trepidation. This response was unsurprising, however, perhaps even understandably rueful, if he had heard the garda view that if he had pleaded guilty to the manslaughter of his wife and not clung to his lies, he would, in all probability, have received a mere two years or so. Lillis now became a watchword, a kind of shorthand for anything from excessive media attention, to lightness in sentencing, to perceived failures in the legal system itself.

Media coverage continued, and, for want of anything to say about Lillis himself, now that he was safely in the relative privacy of Wheatfield Prison, his financial matters rose to great importance. The fact that he was due to get half of his wife's assets had already been in the news, although there were frequent stories about the possibility of legal action by the Cawley family to prevent this from happening. The press had settled into a holding pattern of stock stories that were absolutely true but in reality said very little apart from speculation and theorizing.

A few days after the sentence hearing, one of the papers who had covered the trial was brought before Justice White when it was discovered they had printed the name of Lillis's daughter during the trial. The *Evening Herald* had already fallen on this legal point and had been ordered to pay equal amounts to one foreign charity and one domestic one. Since it was days after the devastating earthquake in Haiti, the foreign half of the money was to be paid to a charity involved in the relief effort. It was a matter for the *Herald* to decide how much should be paid. The latest offender was the *Sunday Mirror*. The girl had been named despite the rigorous warnings that been given to the press on an almost daily basis in the early days of the trial. Once again, Justice White left it up to the paper to decide their own punishment, and, like the *Herald*, they were ordered to split their penance with half to a domestic charity and half to help the victims of the Haiti quake.

Jean Treacy, too, continued to make the newspaper headlines, given that a picture of her would still guarantee a front page. She became a virtual recluse, hiding from the constant attention that was now trained on her. It was widely reported that her engagement was back on with her boyfriend and that they were planning a summer wedding. Every now and then photographs appeared showing them looking strained and tired on the occasional trips they made outside the house. As her shielding by the gardaí on her single court appearance continued to be debated in columns, blogs and editorials, the reasons why she might have worried about her privacy were clear for all to see.

Elsewhere, friends of Celine Cawley had leapt to her defence in response to the negative image of her that had emerged during the trial. Quotes gathered in the days after her death were used again, and other sources were found that showed her in a more positive light. Friends and ex-boyfriend all chipped in. Her cousin and best friend, Juliette Hussey, gave several interviews to put the record straight. She told the *Sunday Independent* that the description of Celine as a 'ball breaker' presented by both sides during the trial was unfair.

'If a woman does well in a professional capacity in law, in justice, in medicine nobody makes any comment. If a woman does well in business those comments are made. Celine was incredibly hard working and very able. She was just incredibly good at what she did. If a woman is good at something – particularly in business – there seems to be people taking swipes.'

Ms Hussey pointed out that the Celine the family knew was not the one that had been portrayed in court, outside of Susanna Cawley's victim impact statement.

'She just made life fun. When we went to France, there was such excitement at spending time with her. She was incredibly good, incredibly kind and generous to the children. She always anticipated what they wanted to do as well. She was the one who would suggest going to the water park, going go-karting, things she knew would give them great enjoyment.'

Ms Hussey said that Celine was happy with her life.

'At the time of her death, she had reached a contented

place in her life. She built up a very successful business which was doing very well. She had an excellent reputation. She worked very hard. She loved spending time in her home in France. And I don't think she would have planned on doing anything terribly different from that.'

Celine's immediate family stayed silent. They at least went largely unmolested as they picked up the pieces of their shattered lives and settled down to their grief. A few weeks after Lillis was sent to jail, a brief mention in the probate courts clarified one matter of Celine's estate. It was reported that Lillis had written from prison relinquishing his role as executor of his wife's will – a legal nicety that was unusual enough to catch media attention with a genuine news line. Her brother and sister took his place and retreated once more into their seclusion.

Slowly the stories became less frequent and papers turned their attention to other news. In March, Lillis once again hit the headlines when probate papers revealed the contents of Celine's will. Headlines appeared that her daughter would be receiving a €1 million nest egg when she turned eighteen at the end of the year. She would inherit the net value of her mother's estate, some €1,059,988.06. The will had been drawn up in 1993, just two years after Celine had married Lillis and when their daughter was only a baby. Toytown Films was still in its infancy when she sat down with her father and her sister Susanna, then a trainee solicitor. Wanting to provide for her young family, she had originally willed everything to her husband, if he was to survive her. The media reports honed in on the section that left Lillis all the property the couple owned 'for his own use absolutely'. The standard legal phrases aimed at providing for the family left behind were lent an added poignancy by the knowledge of the brutal dissolution of that marriage. Lillis was to be the will's executor, and the assets would only pass to the children that were still dreamed of if both parents had died.

It was a standard document but the dry legal terminology could not blot out the gruesome interest in its implications. Lillis might have surrendered his role as executor but the media reports all added that his daughter would now receive her bequest because Lillis had lost his right to it once he was convicted of killing her mother. Under the 1965 Succession Act he was barred from inheriting once convicted. However, the media reports were eager to remind the reading public that he would still benefit financially from his wife's death. He would receive his half of the value of the couple's three houses, including the French holiday home that Celine had so loved. He would also still get his half of the sale of Toytown Films, a figure in the region of €350,000. The total of what he stood to receive was widely estimated to be around the €2 million mark.

After the trauma of the trial and the glare of the media spotlight they could only now wait for the dust to settle and life to resume some form of normality. As Susanna Cawley had written in her victim impact statement, their concern was now with Celine's daughter who would have only a few more months of anonymity before her long awaited eighteenth birthday stripped away that legal protection. Whether or not she would still celebrate her birthday with the lavish party it had been reported her father was planning before he was sent to prison was unclear, but it was certain that she would always have to live with what had happened on that morning in December 2008.

Windgate Road itself settled back into its suburban calm. Lillis sent letters to each household, apologizing for the upheaval caused in their lives. The high gates remained closed that bit more securely and the glances when residents met a stranger on the road might be more suspicious, but for the most part life returned to normal. Photographers no longer camped out in the narrow laneway beside Rowan Hill and the news vans no longer parked along the leafy road. Rowan Hill itself remained aloof behind its high wooden gates, waiting for a time when there, too, life could continue.

MORE TRUE CRIME FROM
THE O'BRIEN PRESS

AFRAID OF THE DARK
The Tragic Story of Robert Holohan
Ralph Riegel

The disappearance of eleven-year-old Robert Holohan on
4 January 2005 touched the hearts of the nation. For eight
days people from all over Ireland searched for the boy. Their
hopes were dashed when his body was found.

Then the full tragedy emerged when his good friend and
neighbour, Wayne O'Donoghue, who had taken part in the
search, was charged with the killing. At his trial he pleaded
guilty to manslaughter and was sentenced to four years in
prison.

DEATH IN DECEMBER
The Story of Sophie Toscan du Plantier
Michael Sheridan

In December 1996 the body of French filmmaker Sophie Toscan du Plantier was discovered outside her remote holiday home near Schull in West Cork, brutally battered to death. The savage murder created shock waves in France and in the quiet Cork countryside she had chosen as a retreat from her high-flying lifestyle.

Despite extensive investigations, the killer of Sophie is still at large – the file remains open.

Based on exclusive interviews with Sophie's parents and her husband, as well as her diaries and family photographs, the book builds a picture of a woman of character – independent, beautiful and fearless. Following the trail of the investigators, it also creates a chilling psychological profile of a sadistic killer.

Also contains a day-by-day account of the Ian Bailey libel trial.

LIFE SENTENCE
Murder Victims and their Families
Catherine Cleary

A teenage boy is snatched as he walks near his house, and beaten to death; a wife and mother is attacked and murdered on a quiet country road; two psychiatric patients are stabbed in sheltered accommodation; a young girl is killed in her own bedroom ...

Death in any circumstances is devastating, but when the cause is murder, grief takes on an extra dimension.

Those left behind live under a life sentence, condemned to years of painful memories and deep regrets.

Based on personal interviews with victims' families, journalist Catherine Cleary tells the horrific stories of twelve murders and how the families have survived their ordeal.

THE BLACK WIDOW
The Catherine Nevin Story
Niamh O'Connor

The best-selling story of Catherine Nevin, the woman who wanted it all and was willing to kill to get it.

When Tom Nevin was brutally murdered, none seemed as grief-stricken as his widow, Catherine. She stood by the graveside holding a single red rose: the classic symbol of a lost love. But there was a lot more to Catherine Nevin than met the eye.

Four years later she stood in the dock, accused of murdering her husband. The trial kept the country enthralled, as every day more bizarre stories emerged: contract killers, money laundering, the IRA, sexual affairs. An incredible story of a cold, calculating woman and her desire for money, power and prestige.